Wrocław

WOI 8322

Janusz Czerwiński

Wrocław

The Silesian Metropolis on the Odra

Photo on front cover: town houses in the market square, G. Gräfenhain/Superbild
Cartography: RV Reise- und Verkehrsverlag GmbH, Berlin · Gütersloh · Leipzig · Munich · Potsdam · Stuttgart 1993
Illustrations: Stefan Arczyński, Wrocław: p. 90, 91, 92, 94/95, 96; Krystyna Gorazdowska, Zakopane: p. 28/29; Stanisława i Krzysztof Jabłońscy, Warsaw: p. 39. 40. 47. 54; Stanisław Klimek, Wrocław: p. 6/7, 15, 18, 19, 21, 23, 25, 27, 31, 33, 35, 41, 43, 44, 45, 48, 49, 51, 53, 55, 56, 57, 59, 61, 63, 66, 67, 68, 69, 71, 73, 75, 76, 79, 80, 82/83, 84, 85, 86; University Library Wrocław: p.16/17

Author: Dr. Janusz Czerwiński, Wrocław
English Translation: Olga Słuckin, Warsaw
Idea and series conception: Prisma Verlag GmbH, Munich
Editing, coordination: Prisma Verlag GmbH, Munich, with the assistance of GeoCenter International Warsaw
Cover layout: Prisma Verlag GmbH, Munich

Typesetting: Buchmacher Bär, Freising
Reproduction: Printex, Verona
Printing and finish: Łódzkie Zakłady Graficzne

ISBN 3-575-26076-1

Contents

SZCZEPIN
STARE
MIASTO
Odra
Kępa Mieszczańska
Ogródki działkowe
Długa
Legnicka
Strzegomska
Braniborska
Grabiszyńska
Podwale
Zaporoska
Swobodna
R.Dmowskiego
Mieszczańska
Most Sikorskiego
Kazimierza Wielkiego
Józefa Piłsudskiego
Powstańców Śląskich
Pomorska
Nowy Świat
Świdnicka
Gajowicka
Rybacka
Rynek Szczepiński
Pl. Strzegomski
Robotnicza
Tęczowa
pl.Orląt Lwowskich
Wrocław

OŁBIN
Nowowiejska
kard. Stefana Wyszyńskiego
Jedności Narodowej
Henryka Sienkiewicza
Bolesława Drobnera
Bolesława Prusa
Odra
Most Grunwaldzki
Pl. Grunwaldzki
Marii Skłodowskiej-Curie
Most Pokoju
Oławska
Romualda Traugutta
Kazimierza Pułaskiego
Małachowskiego
Wrocław Główny
Sucha
Dyrekcyjna
Hubska
Krakowska
Oława
Park Nowowiejski
Politechnika Wrocławska
Ogród Botaniczny
Muzeum Przyrodnicze
Muzeum Archidiecezjalne
Katedra
Ostrów Tumski
Wyspa Piasek
Wyspa Słodowa
Wyspa Bielarska
Muzeum Narodowe
Rotunda Panoramy Racławickiej
Muzeum Architektury
al. Juliusza Słowackiego
Pl. Powstańców Warszawy
Pl. Społeczny
Park Wschodni
KKS "Polonia"
Ogródki działkowe
Na Grobli
Wybrzeże Stanisława Wyspiańskiego
Akademia Rolnicza
Pl. Dominikański
Pl. Konstytucji 3 Maja
Kościuszki
Tadeusza Kościuszki
Pogotowie Ratunkowe
Na Niskich Łąkach
Żabia Ścieżka
Szpital kliniczny
Pl. Katedralny
Pl. Westerplatte
Piastowska
Grunwaldzka
Szczytnicka

Above: Façade of a house in Słodowa Street; engraving by Henry Mützel, 1827.
Page 2: Statue of the Fencer; Hubert Lederer, 1903.
Page 6/7: Panorama of Wrocław.

Town History

Wrocław is a town of particular beauty and specific atmosphere resulting from the heritage of a thousand-year history rich in events of often a tragical nature. It is a border town for three nations and for a number of different cultures, which have manifested their presence in Wrocław's material and spiritual face, in its architecture and art, and in its tradition and adherence to a common system of values.

Wrocław's roots reach back to distant times. The first settlements situated within the present area of the town were built on the banks of the Odra where the roads running along the river met. The centuries-old route leading from the south of Europe to the Baltic also ran along here making use of shallows and islands to overcome the problems caused by the numerous arms of a river flowing through a wide and marshy valley. The area, inhabited from Neolithic times by agricultural tribes of various cultures, became the place of settlement for the Slavonic tribe of the Slezans, who were later incorporated into the Grand Moravian State and, after its fall, into the Czech State. The name of the biggest stronghold, which had existed on the island from at least the 7th century, derived from the Czech sovereign Vratislav I (d. 921), but was later changed to Ostrów Tumski. Like the rest of the Silesian lands, the settlement was incorporated into Poland, then ruled by Mieszko I from the Piast dynasty, around the year 990.

At the turn of the 11th century the strategically important stronghold was extended to become one of the royal seats. Its role grew markedly after the foundation, in 1000, of the Wrocław bishopric and the construction of a stronghold for the bishop, with a cathedral in its centre. From that time on Wrocław became Silesia's political, administrative and religious centre. In the 12th century a further two settlements were founded. One, belonging to governor Peter Włostowic, was situated close to his residence on the Ołbina, with the St Vincent's Benedictine Abbey, founded by him around 1139, in the neighbourhood. The other settlement was located on the left and higher bank of the Odra (near the present seat of the university), where an old trade route crossed the river. It ran from

Panorama of Wrocław, from the »Liber Chronicarum«, 1493.

Leipzig and Legnica to Opole and Cracow, and on to Kievian Russia, with which lively contacts were already established at the time. The role of that route greatly increased after Cracow became the capital of Poland.

After years of inner unrest and wars between the Czech dynasty of Premyslid, Polish Piasts and Roman Empire rulers for influence in Silesia, a period of political stability, favourable for the economic expansion of Silesia and Wrocław, began in the 13th century. The town, referred to in 1209 as *civitas*, remained one of the main centres of political and cultural life in the country. Henry I the Bearded (1201–38) and his son Henry II the Pious (fell 1241 in the battle of Legnica against the Mongols) both ruled over a considerable part of ethnically Polish land and strove for the royal crown. Their endeavours, especially for the economy (colonization of Silesian land with settlers from the West, founding of monasteries, support of trade and crafts), did not, however, result in the expected unification of Poland, consolidating, instead, separatism in Silesia. Only the Church maintained lasting links with the rest of the Polish territory – until 1821 the Silesian bishops were

under the control of the arch-bishop of Gniezno. The Church also played a significant role in creating the spiritual and cultural reputation of the developing Wrocław. Monks were summoned from Western Europe and from Bohemia, and the monasteries founded by them became important centres that propagated the Western ways of life, especially in culture and art. Following the example of the Benedictines (later Premonstrants), who founded their abbey on the Ołbina before 1139, the Augustinians moved to Wrocław from the nearby Sobótka in 1150; the Franciscans were the first to build a monastery in Poland (1235). In 1222 the Dominicans arrived in Wrocław from Cracow, and soon after nuns moved to richly endowed convents: the St Claire Sisters in 1253, the Dominican Sisters in 1290, the Augustinians in 1299, and others.

Soon the stronghold on the Ostrów Tumski island, with the castle and the two outlying complexes, became too small for the prince's and the bishop's courts. The prince moved his seat to a new castle on the left bank of the Odra, near a rapidly developing settlement. In 1266, still under the rule of Henry I the Bearded, the first location *(prima locatio)* of the town on the left bank took place, in the area of the present Plac Nankera square. Another deed of location was issued in 1241, after the Mongol invasion which proved so destructive for Wrocław. Streets were outlined with a centrally situated market square where the town hall, the cloth hall, the town-scales and the slaughterhouse premises were located. On a square adjacent to the market St Elizabeth's parish church was built and another market place, later known as the Salt Market, was created. Monasteries were built for the Hospitallers (Red-Star Teutonic Knights) at Szewska Street, as well as for the Franciscans and St Claire Sisters at Plac Nankera square, the Dominicans and Dominican Sisters at Św. Katarzyny Street and Plac Dominikański square, and the Augustinians (Eremites), later Franciscans, at Świdnicka Street.

In 1261 Wrocław was granted the Magdeburg city statutes. Two years later the rivalling Nowe Miasto/New Town was founded in the area of the present Nowy Targ/New Market and, in 1337, it was merged with the Old Town into a single urban unit. In the years 1260-70 the entire left-bank part of the town was surrounded by a ring of brick walls with seven gates for protection. The access to the town was defended from the north by the Odra river and on the other sides by the waters of the Oława flowing in a bed specially dug for that purpose. Occupying an area of 133 hectares and inhabited by 14,000 people, Wrocław was one of Central Europe's biggest cities, almost equal to Prague.

From the beginnings of its history Wrocław was differentiated ethnically, culturally and linguistically. Besides by Germans it was inhabited by Poles, Jews, Flemings, Walloons and other nationalities who were merchants or belonged to other trades. The islands on the Odra were the domain of monasteries and of the bishop's court. Very soon Wrocław became a trade centre of European rank, mostly thanks to the privileges granted to it, such as the mile right (1271), the guild right (1273), the warehousing right (1274), etc. From the mid-12th century fairs were held near the monastery of St Vincent on the Ołbin and St John the Baptist's Monastery on the Ostrów Tumski island. By the end of the 12th century market places already existed on Księże Wielkie on the route to Cracow and, from the beginning of the 13th century, in the left-bank part of the town. Later, the biggest of the dozen or so fairs organized every year, the one held in June on the day of John the Baptist, the patron of the town, strengthened the position of the Wrocław townspeople and the rank of Wrocław among the Silesian towns.

The death, in 1336, of Henry VI, the last prince of the Piast dynasty, the political treaties with Luxembourgers established earlier, and the relinquishment by Poland of the dynastic rights to Silesia

Town Hall portal with coat of arms.

(1339) resulted in the incorporation of Wrocław and the Wrocław Duchy into the Czech Kingdom. The period of the rule of Charles IV and of the kings of the Jagiellonian dynasty who ruled the Czechs after him was highly favourable for Wrocław. The town expanded, its wooden houses were replaced by new brick ones. Magnificent Gothic churches were built and the Town Hall was enlarged. Water supply systems were provided, major streets were paved and, in 1378, the construction of new defence walls was started.

In the middle of the fourteenth century Wrocław became an important centre of artistic life, admittedly influenced by Prague but maintaining lively contacts with numerous centres in Western and Eastern Europe, particularly with Cracow where many of Wrocław's younger inhabitants went for academic studies. Wrocław architecture reached a particularly high level; its Gothic churches, together with even older buildings, luckily saved from war destruction, form one of Europe's most magnificent complexes of sacral architecture. A great number of valuable paintings, as well as stone and wood sculptures and examples of artistic craft have survived up to our times to be admired now in churches and in the collections of the Archdiocesan Museum and the National Museum.

Wrocław, 1745; from »Vratislavia Antiquissima et Celeberrima ducat«.

ODER
Neue Statt
ODER

Romanesque portal in the Benedictine Abbey on the Ołbina.

In the 15th century a number of long and highly devastating wars were fought in Silesia (1420–34), in which the Wrocław patritiate held the side of the opponents to Hussitism. Later, having refused to recognize the rule of George of Podibrady and, proclaiming itself in favour of Maciej Korwin, the king of Hungary, the town had to live through a siege by Polish and Czech armies in 1474. Finally, the Jagiellons in the person of King Louis (1516–26) returned to the Czech throne and their rule was again a happy period for Wrocław. Louis's death in 1526, in the battle of Mohacz

Fragment of the portico in St John the Baptist's Cathedral.

against the Turks, decided the political future of the town which, together with Silesia and the Czech State, came under the rule of the Hapsburgs. In 1527 Wrocław paid homage to Ferdinand I, king of the Czechs and Hungarians and, from 1556, also Emperor of Germany. In 1535 he granted a new coat of arms to the town.

The peaceful period of the first half of the 16th century favoured the development of trade and guild craft. The ideas of the Reformation found their way to the town mainly thanks to Pastor Johann Hess, and gained numerous supporters among the townspeople. Active at the time were such outstanding humanists as Martin Opitz, Angelus Silesius, Andreas Gryphius and others.

In terms of town construction Wrocław, which was restricted in size by its medieval walls, underwent only insignificant changes. The fear of a Turkish invasion was responsible for the liquidation of the influential St Vincent's Abbey on the Ołbina and for the decline of the right-bank part of Wrocław, which practically did not expand until the middle of the 18th century.

The outbreak of the Thirty Years' War (1618–48) stopped the economic development of Wrocław for many years. The fighting in Silesia, the garrisoning of the armies of both fighting sides in the town, contributions and diseases resulted not only in heavy financial losses but also in a massive decrease in Wrocław's population. 13,231 people died in the epidemic in 1633 alone, so that by 1640 the number of inhabitants had dropped by half to only 25,000.

The situation changed only after the conclusion of the Peace of Westphalia and the re-establishment of commercial contacts with Poland – a traditional market for Wrocław handcrafted goods and a source of raw materials, mainly corn, cattle, skins, wool, honey and, obviously, salt. Soon Dresden and Leipzig began to compete with Wrocław on the Polish market, especially during the time of Polish-Saxon personal union in the years 1697–1763.

The reconstruction of Wrocław took place during the period of the Counter-Reformation in the spirit of the Baroque age, inspired by the artistic circles of Prague, Vienna and Munich. Supported by the pro-Catholic Hapsburg court, the monastic orders became very active in the town, especially the Jesuits, who erected the large complex of the Jesuit College with seminary and church on the bank of the Odra. Many other Baroque monasteries and churches were erected at the time and Gothic churches were given Baroque interiors. New brick houses were built on and around the market, as well as a number of magnificent residences with the Hatzfelds' palace in the fore, and the bastion-type fortifications were extended.

This dynamic development of Wrocław was stopped by the war between Prussia and Austria. In August 1741, breaking the promise of respecting Wrocław's neutrality given by Friedrich II, the Prussian army entered the town. The period of the Silesian Wars (1740–42 and 1744–45) and the Seven Years' War (1756–63), which was ended by the Hubertusburg treaty, decided the political future of Silesia and Wrocław, which were annexed by Prussia.

St Idzi's Church, 13th c.

The initial period of the rule of Friedrich the Great was difficult for the town both because of the cancelling of privileges it had possessed from medieval times, and the break of its traditional economic links. Another burden for Wrocław was its transformation into one of Prussia's biggest and strongest fortresses manned with numerous military garrisons. Strong earth bastions were constructed on the Ostrów Tumski and Kępa Mieszczańska islands. Fortifications in the northern and western areas of the town were extended to isolate it from its suburbs where workers' settlements were emerging around the manufacturing plants.

At the turn of the 18th century Wrocław was inhabited by approximately 65,000 people. In December 1806 French troops surrounded the town and, after a short siege and the destruction of the suburbs, they entered the town in January 1807. In 1813 Wrocław became the centre of anti-Napoleonic opposition – this found expression in the famous proclamation by Friedrich Wilhelm III, beginning with the words: »To my nation …«.

In 1808 the structure of the town underwent reforms and in 1810 the church and monasterial estates were secularised – out of fourteen monasteries only three remained. At the same time the medieval town fortifications – walls, ramparts and gates – were demolished to make space for the expansion of the city, especially to the east and south. The walls were replaced by a system of promenades (the »Ring«) with parks and green spaces which were later surrounded by magnificent public buildings and residences. The area of the present Plac Kościuszki square – then the centre of the Świdnickie Przedmieście suburb – had been planned in the French manner.

In the first half of the 19th century, thanks to the economic boom, industry began to develop, mainly through the modernization of the outdated manufacturing plants and craft workshops existing in the town. The source of inspiration for these changes was the first great industrial exhibition in 1832. The approaching industrialization of the town was heralded by the construction, in 1819, of Henckmann's factory of machines for sugar processing, soon after the world's first successful attempt to refine sugar from sugar beet had been undertaken in Silesia. The Gotfryd Linke plant, which started work in 1839 and merged with Ruffer's machine factory in 1897, later became Europe's biggest factory of railway cars under the name of *Linke-Hoffmann-Werke* (today the Pafawag). Several metallurgical plants were also opened including the well-known Archimedes screw and bolt factory (1875).

The food industry, based on the products of Lower-Silesian agriculture, experienced a period of a rapid and important expansion. In the middle of the nineteenth century Wrocław had a tobacco plant, a chocolate factory, four chickory plants, 42 distilleries and 81 breweries. Half of the Wrocław population earned their living in those plants.

The industrial expansion was accompanied by the emergence of various financial and insurance institutions. The Wrocław Exchange began to operate in 1844; and the year 1856 was witness to the foundation of the Silesian Association of Banks (later known as the Wrocław Bills of Exchange Bank), the Land Joint-Stock

Gothic epitaph on the Cathedral wall.

Bank and several private banks, as well as branches of big German banks with the Dresdner Bank and the Commercial Bank in the fore. In the beginning of the 20th century a dozen large banks, including the City Bank, were operating in Wrocław.

To meet the growing needs of the administration, many central-Silesian governmental agencies and offices had to be established in addition to the already existing provincial authorities headed by the President General, such as the Wrocław notary's offices and the headquarters of the VI Army Corps. In 1850, the Direction of Post and in 1884 the Central Railway Board were seated in Wrocław.

The economic expansion was accompanied by an enlivening of cultural life. In 1811 the Jesuit Leopoldine Academy and the Protestant Viadrina University in Frankfurt on the Oder were merged to form the Wrocław University. Among other scientific and cultural societies established at the time, those of historians, including art historians, were particularly active. The result of their efforts was the establishment of the Picture Gallery (1853), the Silesian Museum of Antiquities (1858), the Silesian Museum of Fine Arts (1880), and the Silesian Museum of Arts and Crafts (1889) which later became quite famous. Among numerous libraries, the City Library later became the second-largest in Germany. The opening, in 1863, of the Wrocław Zoo was quite an event; and 1872 witnessed the ceremony of the opening of the City Theatre at Świdnicka Street, rebuilt after a fire.

Wrocław's communal facilities were relatively modern for those times. In 1830, as part of the reconstruction of the old water supply system, iron pipes began to be used; the sewage system was also modernized. It should be borne in mind that, situated on the banks of the Odra and its tributaries on rather level ground, Wrocław faced (and still does) serious problems concerning the drainage of water and sewage. Another achievement was the opening, as early as 1847, of Wrocław's first gas supply plant. Oil lighting was then replaced by gas (still in operation on the Ostrów Tumski island). In 1891 electric lighting was introduced, and the horse-drawn street cars operating since 1876 gave way to electric street cars.

The victorious end of the war against France (1870), followed by high contribution payments, resulted in the inflow of investment capital and the enlivening of the building trade. Many public buildings were built at the time, such as schools and hospitals and, in the years 1890-1907, a complex of university hospitals as well as two grand Neo-Gothic churches – the Catholic St Michael's and the Protestant Luther's (the latter was destroyed in 1945). Wood was replaced by steel elements in the structures of the majority of Wrocław's bridges, from the Most Piaskowy/Sand Bridge (1861) to the most beautiful of Wrocław's bridges, the Most Cesarski/Imperial Bridge, today known as Grunwaldzki Bridge.

Wrocław was the first town on the European continent to plan to have steam railway lines constructed (1816). The plan was put into effect only 25 years later, when the construction of the first section of the Upper-Silesian railway line was started. In May 1842 its first section, from Wrocław to Oława, was opened, and in 1856 a new

Oławska Street. Pen drawing by Henry Mützel, 1826.

central station was built to Grapow's design in connection with the extension of the line to Poznań. Thus, Wrocław obtained direct railway links with, for example, Berlin, Hamburg, Szczecin and Leipzig as well as with Upper Silesia and Cracow, soon becoming one of the biggest and most important railway junctions in Central Europe.

The regulation of the Odra river, started on a grand scale in the second half of the 19th century and accompanied by the construction of canals and ports, improved the transport of goods by water between the industrialized Upper Silesia and the agricultural Lower Silesia on the one hand, and between Baltic and North German harbours on the other. The construction of a system of hydrographic projects (weirs, locks, sluices and polders) effectively safeguarded the town against the disastrous floods of the Odra and its tributaries. Constructed before WW I, the Wrocław Water Junction still remains an interesting example of 19th-century technology.

All these enterprises contributed to a rapid growth of Wrocław's population which, from slightly above 100,000 in 1848, increased to about 208,000 in 1871 and 426,000 in 1900. In the middle of the 19th century Wrocław was already third in size among the towns of the German Reich, after Berlin and Hamburg, only to be later surpassed by Leipzig and Munich and, in 1910, by Dresden and Cologne.

In the 19th century and at the beginning of the 20th, Wrocław was a multi-national and multi-religious town dominated, in terms of the number of inhabitants, by Protestants (57.2%) and Catholics (37.5%); but the Jewish community (20.000 – 4.9% of Wrocław's total population) was the third-largest in Germany as a whole at the end of the 19th century. The commercial and financial institutions of the town were dominated by the Jews. Many were also to be found among university staffs, doctors and lawyers.

Just before the outbreak of WW I, Wrocław's population reached 543,400. After its drop, by 1917, to 494,600, it grew to 528,300 by 1919, 556,800 by 1925, 616,600 in 1930 and nearly 630,000 at the outbreak of WW II. Thus Wrocław was Germany's eighth-largest town in terms of the number of its inhabitants, after Berlin, Hamburg, Cologne, Munich, Leipzig, Dresden and Essen.

The rapid urban expansion of the town, the emergence of new lines of industry, combined with the far-reaching stratification of society, transformed Wrocław's architectural landscape, giving way to manufacturing plants, public buildings, railway stations, ports and, mostly, tall tenement houses with communal green spaces sparsely scattered inbetween them. The spontaneous and rather chaotic house construction, especially in the suburbs, urgently required the city administration to prepare a municipal building plan. Such a plan, developed by the architect M. Sadebeck in 1855-60, created a basis for the building of interesting urban complexes, e.g. in the area of the Central Railway Station, Plac Św. Macieja square, Plac Powstańców Śląskich square and street, etc. Large park areas were created as well, such as Park Szczytnicki and Park Poludniowy. Thanks to the regulation of the Odra it became possible to build two suburban settlements in the formerly marshy valley: Zalesie (1901) and Karłowice (1904), also based on the town-garden-concept.

The Baroque building of Wrocław University.

Such styles as Historicism and, especially, Neo-Gothicism and Neo-Renaissance, which dominated Wrocław's architecture until the end of the 19th and the beginning of the 20th century, gave way to modernism introduced by H. Poelzig and, later, by M. Berg. Buildings constructed for the grand historical exhibition in 1913, particularly the Century Hall (Hala Ludowa – People's Hall), were the greatest achievements of that period.

In 1924 Wrocław already occupied an area of 49.6 sq km. Overpopulation in some of its parts, especially in the city centre, and the poor sanitary conditions in a great number of houses compelled the city authorities to develop another town extension and reconstruction plan. In 1928 the area of Wrocław grew to about 175 sq km. New, architecturally modern settlements were built on the area included into the boundaries of Wrocław, for example Popowice, Sępolno, Biskupin, Pilczyce, Muchobór, Grabiszynek, etc. Vast recreation grounds were created around Park Szczytnicki and, in the 1930s, a big sports complex known as the Olympic Stadium was built to a design by Richard Konwiarz (1927), for which he received a distinction at the Los Angeles Olympic Games in 1932. In the same period the premises of the police headquarters in Podwale Street, the Central Post Office Building at Krasińskiego Street and a building for bank offices on the Market were erected.

Wrocław avant-garde architects (A. Rading, H. Lauterbach and others), very active at that time, organized a great architectural exhibition in 1929 entitled *Wohnung und Werkraum* (House and

Panoramic view of the destroyed Wrocław, 1945.

Workplace) – *Wu-Wa* for short. Many outstanding architects, with Hans Schauron in the lead, were invited to take part in it. Luckily most of the buildings erected according to their designs in the area of Kopernika and Tramwajowa streets and at the borders of Park Szczytnicki survived the war.

The gaining of power by Hitler and the rule of the national socialists caused a mass exodus of Jews from Wrocław as early as 1933. In 1938 the big historical synagogue situated at the present Łąkowa street was burnt down. The Poles (about 20,000 of them lived in Wrocław at the time) also suffered Nazi repressions, in the form of the expulsion of Polish students from Wrocław University, and in other forms. In view of the approaching war, industrial plants switched over to the production of military equipment including tanks. The troops of the VIII Army commanded by General Blaskowitz were concentrated in Wrocław.

After the outbreak of WW II Polish prisoners of war and compulsory workers were brought to Wrocław to work in the industrial plants (after the end of the war they became the town's first Polish settlers). Since Wrocław was situated at almost equal distance from the western and eastern front lines, and since the town stayed beyond the reach of allied aircraft bombing, many people from Central Germany and Berlin sought refuge there, increasing the number of Wrocław's inhabitants to one million. The progress of events on the eastern and western fronts, decisive for the final fate of the war, strengthened the determination of the Nazi administration in Wrocław. In August 1944 the town was declared the *Festung Breslau* – a closed stronghold.

When the offensive of the 1st Ukrainian Front of the Soviet Army began in January 1945, Wrocław's Gauleiter K. Hahnke ordered the evacuation of nearly 700,000 civilians, mainly old men, women and children, as being of no use for the defence of the town. 200,000 Wroclavians were permitted to stay, plus war prisoners, compulsory workers and about 65,000 soldiers in the garrison. The dramatic evacuation of people from Wrocław to West Germany during a very cold winter resulted in many deaths. By mid-February 1945, the siege ring around Wrocław had been closed; but the seizing of the town by the Red Army, planned for only 3-4 days, took much longer. Twice – at the end of February and March – Wrocław was stormed by Soviet troops supported by heavy artillery, however not from the north and east, as was expected, but from the west and south. As a result, the parts of Wrocław situated in those areas suffered heaviest destruction. The city centre experienced continuous fire by heavy artillery and bombing from the air. To defend the city centre and to widen the field of firing for German artillery, the order was given to burn and demolish entire housing districts in that area. A field airport was created on the site of the present Plac Grunwaldzki square.

On May 6, 1945, four days after the fall of Berlin, and after 80 days of siege, General H. Niehoff, Commander of the *Festung Breslau*, signed the act of capitulation, thus ending the drama of the town and its inhabitants. Approximately 170,000 civilians died in the course of evacuation or were killed during the siege. 6,000 German officers and soldiers fell, 24,000 were wounded and 40,000 were taken prisoner. The losses of the Red Army amounted to 736 officers and over 7,000 soldiers.

The Neo-Gothic Court Building.

Wrocław emerged from the war in an almost completely destroyed state except for its residential suburbs. Out of a total number of 30,000 houses about 21,600, that is 70%, mostly public buildings including 400 historical buildings, were in ruins. What has happened to many priceless pieces of art from Wrocław museums (none of which avoided war destruction) remains unknown. No one knows the fate of the *Golden Treasure of Wrocław,* deposited in its banks. This is what Rev. Paul Peikert from St Maurice's parish wrote in his »Chronicle of the days of siege. Wrocław 22.1.-6.5.1945«: »(...) Magnificent, ancient churches, God's earthly shrines, the holy places of sacrifice (...) present a picture of destruction and ruin. This much is left of Wrocław, the once so beautiful, splendid town on the banks of the Odra ...«.

As a result of the territorial changes that followed the defeat in the war and the fall of the Third Reich, Silesia and Wrocław were included into the territory of Poland. The Poles accepted this fact as their return to the Piast land and the restoration to Poland of the heritage ruled by Mieszko I and Bolesław Chrobry in the 10th and 11th centuries; whereas for the Germans it was an annexation of land by those who had won the war.

After the end of the hostilities, the displacement of Germans still living in Wrocław was started, their place being gradually taken by Poles expelled from the territories lost by Poland in the East, or streaming in from other regions of the country that had suffered heavy destruction in the war, as well as by compulsory workers and prisoners returning from the camps in Germany.

In 1945 already work was started on the removal of ruins and debris and the repairing of communal facilities such as water, gas and electric power supply systems, street car lines and the reconstruction of industrial plants. The rebuilding of bridges enabled the re-opening of railway and road traffic to the right-bank part of Wrocław, less destroyed and filled with people immediately after the end of the hostilities. January 1946 was witness to the opening of the Pafawag railway car factory (formerly *Linke-Hoffmann Werke*). A railway line ending in the centre of the city helped to remove debris from there. Architects and building contractors concentrated on the securing and reconstruction of the most valuable historical buildings, first of all those testifying the the Polish, Piast roots of the town. At the time this was a political and emotional factor very important for the integration of the ethnically, socially and financially diversified society in its new, strange place of settlement; a society burdened with the memory of tragic war experiences, a society remembering the wrongs done to them.

The Baroque statue of St John Nepomucen.

The main problem faced by the post-war authorities was to provide the inflowing settlers with roofs over the heads and workplaces – a very difficult task in view of their tremendous range of destruction suffered by the town and the country as a whole. Help from the state administration was out of the question – Warsaw, Gdańsk and many other smaller and bigger towns throughout Poland were in a similar situation. Nevertheless, the enthusiasm of the pioneers, together with the determination and combined efforts of the people of Wrocław resulted in the restoration of the town to the role of a centre of economic and cultural life for Lower Silesia. Today Wrocław, with some 650,000 inhabitants, is Poland's fourth largest town and a centre of the transport industry, as well as of the electrical engineering, electronic, chemical, textile and food industry, amongst others.

Wrocław's intellectual potential is growing constantly thanks to the thirteen academic schools located there, with more than 30,000 students. Cultural life is blooming, and in the cultural panorama of the town the activities within theatre, music and fine arts are impressive. The extension of the city's technological infrastructure including central heating, water supply and sewage treatment plants, along with the modernization of the outdated and inefficient city transport system has been undertaken, as the town has been expanding, expecially to the west, north and south. Within the framework of this process the suburbs, such as Popowice, Gądów, Nowy Dwór, Kozanów, Maślice and Zakrzów, are gradually being transformed into modern housing settlements. This is accompanied by the reconstruction of the city centre where, on a scale unexperienced in Poland so far, dwelling houses and public buildings featuring new, unconventional architecure are being constructed.

On the threshold of the 21st century, under new, transformed political and social conditions, Wrocław is facing a new challenge and new chances are being opened through its historical heritage and its unique position in a Europe which is progressing along the road towards integration.

Wrocław today, a bird's eye view.

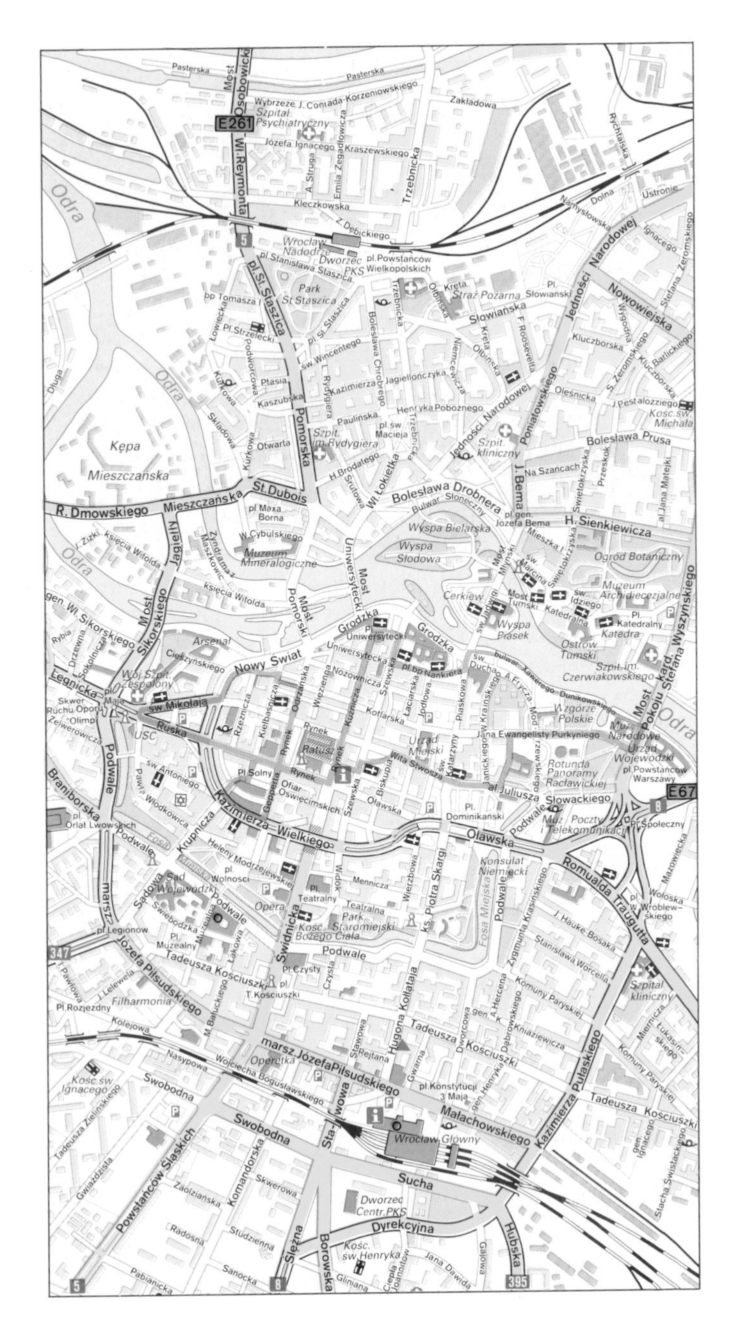

Walk
Old Town and New Town

Market • Town Hall • The Griffon House • The Vasa Court • The House of the Seven Electors • Plac Solny The Old Exchange • Kazimierza Wielkiego Street St Elisabeth's Church • Stare Jatki • Arsenal • Ruska Street • Św. Mikołaja Street • Market • The Golden Crown House • Kuźnicza Street • University • University Church of the Blessed Name of Jesus • Ossolineum St Vincent's Church • Market Hall • National Museum Racławicka Panorama • St. Adalbert's Church Wita Stwosza Street • St Mary Magdalene's Church

The Wrocław **Market**, a vast square occupying 3.7 hectares (208x175 m), outlined when Wrocław became subject to the Magdeburg statutes in 1241, has preserved its old layout which made it a crossing point for eleven streets and passages. The centre of the square is occupied by the Town Hall and several houses erected in place of the demolished cloth-hall and merchant stalls. The Neo-Gothic City House (1860–63) accommodates the »U Spiża« beer cellar in its basement. In the northern part of the Market several old, mainly Baroque and classicistic houses, some remodelled in the 19th and 20th centuries, have survived.

The **Town Hall** ranks among the most superb in Central Europe. Its construction was begun at the end of the 13th century, and was continued until the 16th century; the result is its present form, partly Gothic and partly Renaissance. After the rebuilding of the upper part of the clock tower in the middle of the 16th century, its Renaissance open-work cupola was roofed with copper sheet. In the 17th century the interior of the Town Hall was totally reconstructed and its western entrance received a Baroque portal. In 1885–90 the Town Hall underwent complete renovation. The gaps in its sculptural decorations on the southern façade were then filled. Conservatory work was continued in 1924–28, 1934–36, 1937–38 and immediately after the end of WW II, to remove the

The route of the walk is marked in grey in the map opposite.

traces of destruction. The interior, regrettably stripped of its original fittings, was adapted to the needs of the Historical Museum located therein.

The visitors' attention is gripped by the striking eastern façade of the Town Hall with the beautifully decorated top section and the astronomical clock underneath, the Gothic bay window of the former city chapel and the eastern Gothic entrance portal. Of equally striking beauty is the southern façade which is partitioned by projections and bay windows and decorated with geometric, plant and figural forms and repeated motifs of the city coat of arms (the Czech lion, the Silesian eagle and the head of St John the Baptist). The two friezes show carved genre scenes. Here is also the entrance to Wrocław's oldest Piwnica Świdnicka (Świdnicka Cellar – 15th c.) – its name is derived from the very popular Świdnickie beer that was served there. Above the entrance one can see two characteristic stone figures – a townswoman and her drunken husband.

Worth seeing is also the interior of the Town Hall (entrance on the western side) and the collections of the Historical Museum located therein. The ground floor is occupied by the vast double-aisled Townspeople Hall connected with the old Court Room and the Council Hall (splendid Renaissance portal, 1528, and inlaid door, 1563), the Council Office and the Governor's Office and Hall. The triple-aisled Grand Hall on the first floor, also known as the Knights' Hall (mid-14th c.) with superb ribbed vault (15th c.) – the representative city hall where ceremonies, receptions and balls are held – is adjacent to the Gothic Prince's Hall, which is supported by a single pillar, with a unique cross-and-ribbed vault and a fine Gothic portal. Built around 1345, the hall fulfilled the role of town hall chapel until the period of the Reformation, and in 1620–1740 that of conference hall for the Silesian states. On the southern side it adjoins the Mayor's Office and the old Treasury Room, both with the original vaults and other Gothic stone elements.

In front of the Town Hall, at its south-eastern corner, one can see a stone pillory, a true replica of the original from 1492, which was destroyed in 1945. The statue of Count Aleksander Fredro, the well-known Polish comedy writer, brought here from Lvov in 1956, has taken the place of the monument to Friedrich Wilhelm, which was removed in 1945 from the small square (once known as the Fish Market) on the western side of the Town Hall. The tall poplar beside it was planted in 1948 by the mayors of Brno and Wrocław as a symbol of Polish-Czech friendship.

The Wrocław Town Hall.

The Town Hall and the buildings occupying the centre of the Market divide it into four parts. The largest, western part is traditionally called Targ Wełny (Wool Market), although as early as the 19th century it was the place of military parades and public meetings. The Large Scales' building, which stood here until 1846, was replaced by a statue of Frederick the Great (A. Kiss, 1847), which in turn was removed from there in 1945.

The buildings in the western part of the Market are in the best condition and are architecturally the most interesting. At No. 2 there stands the biggest merchant house, **Pod Gryfami/The Griffon House**, built in 1587–89 by F. Gross and G. Hendrik in Dutch mannerism style, with a fascinating Late-Renaissance portal and a

Houses on the western part of the Market.

coat of arms cartouche. No. 4 is the Pod Złotym Orłem/The Golden Eagle, a Baroque stone house (1st half of the 18th c.) with embedded portal (1707) taken from the demolished Schreyfogel Palace. No. 5, the **Dwór Wazów/Vasa Court**, built in Gothic style (its original cellars now accommodate a winetavern), was rebuilt in 1574 in Renaissance style. Recently reconstructed, it now houses a restaurant and the Wiedeńska/Viennese Café. No. 6 is the stylish Baroque house Pod Złotym Słońcem/The Golden Sun, built around 1727, with a gorgeous portal and lovely interior accommodating the exhibitions of the Medal Engraving Museum, the bookshop of the Wrocław Ossolineum Publishing House and, in the outbuildings, a modern art gallery. No. 7, called Pod Niebieskim Słońcem/The Blue Sun, erected in the 14th century and later remodelled a couple of times, served for a long time as an inn for kings and princes visiting Wrocław. No. 8, the **Pod Siedmioma Elektorami/House of the Seven Electors** is one of the oldest in Wrocław. Built in the 13th century, and rebuilt in the 14th century, in 1503 and 1672 respectively, it has a pillar-type portal adorned with a Hapsburg eagle. The partly preserved façade shows the effigies of several electors, with Emperor Leopold I in the centre.

Gothic vault in the Grand Hall of the Town Hall.

The corner house (No. 9/11) is a ten-storey bank office building (1929–31, architect H. Rump) erected within the framework of an ambitious project (luckily abandoned) to reconstruct the market in a modernistic style.

An auxiliary market place on the south-western side of the Market is known as **Plac Solny/Salt Square** or Plac Polski/Polish Square. Between the end of the 19th century and 1945 its name was Blücher Square. Today it is a popular flower market. Among the old houses which surround it, mostly reconstructed after 1945, the most striking is the grand, classicistic **Stara Giełda/Old Exchange**, erected in 1822–24 to the design of the outstanding architect K. P. Langhans. At the corner of the Ofiar Oświęcimskich and Gepperta streets one can see the Rybisch House (reconstructed) with a beautiful Renaissance portal from 1531.

A narrow passage leads from the corner of Plac Solny to a back lane where the Szajnochy and Psie Budy streets meet the Plac Bohaterów Getta square, formerly the centre of Wrocław's Jewish district. The reconstruction of this part of Wrocław in the 19th century and, particularly, after WW II, changed its appearance, eliminating the mostly wooden houses tightly squeezed along a canal of the Oława river whose waters propelled corn mills and sawmills. No. 10, Szajnochy Street is the old palace of the Wallenberg-Pachaly family, built in 1787 by K. G. Langhans in early classicistic style. Here, Goethe stayed during his trip to Silesia in 1790. The Neo-Gothic building (1887–89) next to it, once the seat of the Rehdigeranum City Library, now houses a large collection of books and the main reading room of the University Library. The Bohaterów Getta Square (known as Żydowski/Jewish Square until 1826 and as Karola IV/Charles IV Square until 1945) is linked with the recently constructed Old Town Ring Road (**Kazimierza Wielkiego Street**); here one can see the Late-Baroque Evangelical Providence Church, formerly a castle church.

The adjacent northern wing of the former Spätgen Palace was rebuilt by K. G. Langhans to form Frederick the Great's residence. A part of the palace, reconstructed after WW I, accommodates the Archeological Museum and Ethnographic Museum. Situated in the short Św. Antoniego (St Anthony's) Street branching off from the Bohaterów Getta Square towards the west, is the Early-Baroque St Anthony's Church, built in 1685 by M. Biener and, beside it, the former Franciscan monastery, taken over in 1792 by the Elizabethan Sisters and, finally, in 1946 by the Salezians. It is situated next to the old Pod Białym Bocianem (The White Stork) synagogue, which is in a poor, dilapidated state.

Plafond in the representative hall of the Golden Sun House.

Walking back to the Market, towards its north-western corner we see two smallish houses at the crossing of the Odrzańska and Św. Mikołaja streets: Jaś (Hansel) (16th c.) and Małgosia (Gretel) (18th c.), a bit bigger, standing at the end of the complex of buildings surrounding what was once a graveyard with a church in the centre.

St Elizabeth's Church, one of the oldest in Wrocław, is presently the third tallest building in Stare Miasto (Old Town). Before the location of Wrocław in 1241 it was a Romanesque church;

Count Alexander Fredro's statue on the Market.

but as early as 1245 it was mentioned as a parish church. In 1253 – 1525 the church was in the hands of the Order of the Knights of the Red Star. Later, until 1945, it was a Protestant church; today it fulfils the role of a military garrison church. Work on its extension, which continued from the middle of the 14th century to the beginning of the 15th century, resulted in giving it the form of a magnificent triple-aisled basilica, one of Silesia's biggest Gothic churches. The nave is 66 m long, 10 m wide and 30 m high. The compact look of its silhouette is emphasized by a ring of side

University Church of the Blessed Name of Jesus, eastern façade.

chapels hidden between the buttresses, with lean-to roofs covering the relieving arches. The massive quadrilateral tower, erected in 1452–58 by master H. Bertold and initially crowned with a slim 128 m high spire covered with a lead-sheet roof, was the highest in Wrocław and Silesia at the time. Destroyed by a storm in 1529 (this story and the following legend are shown on the wall reliefs), the spire was replaced by a fine Renaissance dome in 1531–35, which unfortunately was destroyed by fire in 1975. In another fire in 1976 the basilica roof and part of the interior were destroyed, including the priceless Baroque organ, the largest in Silesia, the work of M. Engler (1750–51), with beautiful wood carvings by J. A. Siegwitz. The church is still under reconstruction. As befits a parish church serving the well-off middle-class inhabitants of Wrocław, its interior is adorned with many valuable objects – outstanding pieces of Silesian and European art – such as Gothic and Renaissance altars including the high altar by master H. Pleydenwurff (around 1470), presently in the Warsaw National Museum; the Late-Gothic stone sacramentarium by J. Tauchen (1455), a Wrocław sculptor, also the creator of sculptures in the Town Hall; the manneristic pulpit (1652) and, most importantly, the Renaissance and Baroque tombs and epitaphs (more than 370 in all), of a high artistic level, both inside and outside the church walls. Amongst them are tombs of the Wrocław humanist H. Rehdiger and his wife (ca. 1585); the monumental Baroque tomb of Jan Jerzy Wolff, senator and imperial councillor (ca. 1772 by famous architect J. B. Fischer von Erlach); the tomb of Henry Rybisch (d. 1544), an outstanding Silesian humanist.

The western part of the Old Town, traditionally called Przedmieście Mikołajskie (Nicolaus Suburb), enclosed within the region of the Ruska, Św. Mikołaja, Kiełbaśnicza, Rzeźnicza, Białoskórnicza and Nowy Świat streets, is presently undergoing wide-scale rebuilding work to restore it to its old appearance. One of the side streets, the **Stare Jatki/Old Shambles** is being turned into an area of art and craft workshops. Nearby, on the Odra bank, in the area of Cieszyńskiego Street, is the **Arsenal Miejski/Old Town Arsenal** (15th c.) and, at Św. Mikołaja Street, the ancient St Barbara's Church in Gothic style (15th–16th c.) – today the Orthodox Church of the Birth of the Blessed Virgin. The reconstruction of this part of the town, which was effected in the 19th century, completely changed its architectural look – once deeply rooted in the Middle Ages – by introducing new historicist and art nouveau elements as is exemplified by houses in such streets as Rzeźnicza and Ruska renowned in the past for their inns and pubs and, later, for elegant stores.

The **Ruska** and **Św. Mikołaja streets** end in 1 Maja Square, one of Wrocław's main traffic junctions. In the underground passage one can see the remnants of the old Mikołajska Gate and an 18th-century bastion. On the southern side of the square, right above the city moat, a stone fountain with Struggle and Victory, allegorical figures representing the fighting Hercules (1905, E. Seger, L. Sehring), can be seen.

The southern, heavily destroyed part of the **Market** was carefully reconstructed in 1949–58. Among the few houses from the 19th century and the beginning of the 20th century which survived in only slightly changed form, there is the Art Nouveau corner building No. 13, from 1904, with rich architectural details. The Pod Starą Szubienicą/Old Gallows House (No. 19), with its old Gothic and Renaissance interior preserved, accommodates the popular Herbowa tea-room.

Flower market on the Plac Solny Square.

Much more interesting are the buildings on the eastern side of the Market, called Zieloney Rury/Green Tube after a medieval well which once existed here. The entire corner of Oławska Street is occupied by the **Pod Złotą Koroną/Golden Crown House**, which was built in 1521-28 for bishop Jan Turzo as his residence, and is fully reconstructed today. In the row of bank premises and shops the building of the Feniks department store in art nouveau style (1904) and, at No. 39/40, the magnificent Neo-Renaissance Elegance store are of particular interest. Of similar character are the houses in the northern part of the Market – although after numerous reconstructions they have lost much of their former architectural value.

Kuźnicza Street, one of the oldest in town, once connected the Market with the royal castle on the Odra river. Repeatedly reconstructed, it lost its historical character. Its past splendour is recalled by the Pod Srebrnym Hełmem/The Silver Helmet House

The »Jaś« and »Małgosia« houses.

(around 1700) with its rich rococo ornamentation, situated at the outlet of the narrow Igielna Street, which is still waiting for reconstruction. The Baroque building of the former St Joseph's Jesuit seminary (No. 35), built by J. Frisch (1735) and also known as the Steffens House after Henrik Steffens, a physicist and philosopher, today accommodates the Department of Anthropology of the Wrocław University and the Polish Academy of Sciences. A statue of St Catherine, the patroness of scientists, by sculptor J. W. Siegwitz, is placed in the inner yard surrounded by galleries.

Wrocław University, southern façade.

Wrocław owes the foundation of a **university** to the Jesuits who arrived here in 1638, during the period of the Counter Reformation, and opened a grammar school. In 1645 they were granted a privilege to organize a college. In 1702, to reward their endeavours, Emperor Leopold I issued a charter of foundation – the famous »Golden Bull« – for the Leopoldine Academy, thus putting into effect an idea which Ludwig IV the Jagiellon had not been able to implement in 1505 because of the protest of the Jagiellonian University. In 1659 the Jesuits started to develop the devastated and abandoned site of the 13th-century royal castle. First they located their college there and erected a church; in 1728 the corner stone for the premises of the Academy had been embedded. The western wing for the school was ready in 1732. After the demolition, in 1734, of the Imperial Gate, the construction of the eastern, monasterial wing was started. In 1737 the short southern wing was ready to accommodate a laboratory and a pharmacy. The large-scale building work, including the erection of the central and eastern towers, could, however, not be continued because of the outbreak of the war between Prussia and Austria in 1741. The college building was transformed into hospital, prison and, in 1757, into a food store. In 1758 the Jesuits obtained permission to complete the construction of the Academy. Although the order was dissolved in 1773, the Leopoldine Academy continued its work until 1811, when the »Schlesische Friedrich-Wilhelm-Universität« was established in Wrocław. The new university was made up of the departments of philosophy and Catholic theology from the Academy and the departments of Protestant theology, law and medicine from the Viadrina University in Frankfurt on the Oder, which had been dissolved. The Wrocław University, organized to the standards of the Berlin University, soon gained fame and recognition. Among its professors from various periods mention should be made of the economists L. Brentano and W. Sombart; philosopher W. Diltey; linguists A. Hillebrandt, W. Cybulski, W. Nehring and A. H. Hoffmann von Fallersleben; historians T. Mommsen and R. Roepell; mathematician E. Kummer; physicists H. Steffens and G. Kirchhoff; chemist R. Bunsen; astronomer J. G. Gall; zoologists C. T. Siebold and W. Kükenthal; botanists L. Ch. Treviranus and H. Göppert; geologist F. Roemer; geographer J. Partsch; surgeons J. Mikulicz-Radecki, R. Förster, J. E. Purkyne, A. Neisser and others.

The students were mostly of Silesian origin, but quite a lot of them came from Wielkopolska and even from Bohemia and Moravia. The Nazi coup d'etat forced many professors, especially those of Jewish descent, to leave the University; Polish students were also expelled. In the final months of 1945, the University was evacuated and most of its premises suffered war destruction. But it came to life again after the end of hostilities mainly thanks to professors who arrived here from the Jana Kazimierza University in Lvov, which had been taken over by the Soviets. At first, the Wrocław University was a part of the Polytechnic, but later some of its departments were transformed into independent academic schools. Today the Wrocław University with its six departments and nearly 14,000 students is the largest in town.

Facing the Odra river the main University building (Collegium Maximum), which is still under construction, is Wrocław's most superb Baroque building with its 171 m long façade to which the Brama Cesarska/Imperial Gate, which leads from the Old Town right to the University Bridge, forms an axis. The modest decoration of the northern elevation obviously contrasts with the southern façade in which both entrances have been placed. The main (western) entrance leads through a narrow portico with a balcony – its balustrade is adorned with statues by J. A. Siegwitz (1736) personifying the four Cardinal Virtues: Justice, Courage, Moderation and Wisdom. Inside, in the vestibule, you will find the portal of the door-keeper's lodge with a statue of Pallas Athena,

Wrocław University, part of the Leopoldine Hall.

imperial eagles and the Schaffgotsch coat of arms. To the right lies the Oratorium Marianum (still under restoration); on the left the lecture rooms of the former Schola Metaphysices et Logices. The vaults of the grand staircase leading to the first storey are adorned with frescoes by F. A. Scheffler (1734–35) – an apotheosis of the Silesian principalities and states, with the pictures of towns, churches and monasteries shown against a Silesian landscape. The gate building, which contains the eastern entrance, is linked with the church. The ground floor houses the old monasterial pharmacy – today the University Club – with an inlaid door, a portal and a superb ceiling fresco by P. A. Scheffler showing Jesus healing the sick. Both entrances lead to the Leopoldine Hall in the western wing, which you enter through a double oak door decorated with the Piast, Silesian and Jagiellon eagles. The interior of the Hall is striking due to its Baroque glamour: superb architecture, many sculpted figures (1731, F. J. Mangoldt) and illusionistic paintings on the vaults (1732, J. K. Handtke) as well as stucco work (J. Provisore). In the background you can see a slightly raised dais with a pulpit in its centre, and a picture showing Emperor Leopold sitting on the throne, beside him the personifications of Sagacity (Consilio) and Industriousness (Industria), the rejected allegories of Quarrel and Stupidity lying at his feet. On both sides of the dais stand the statues of Leopold's sons (later emperors) Joseph I and Charles VI. The ceiling fresco shows the scenes of the foundation and construction of the University and of it being surrendered into the care of the Virgin Mary. The auditorium is filled with the rows of benches and the professors' stalls under the window. Window bays accommodate the medallion portraits of famous Church philosophers and doctors. The vault is covered with a fresco showing the apotheosis of God's Wisdom. Immediately at the entrance to the hall there is a music gallery supported by pillars and adorned with the bust and coat of arms cartouche of J. A. Schaffgotsch, who was Silesia's General Starost in the period of the construction of the University premises. The vault shows an allegory of Silesia with Silesia sitting in the centre on a throne. In the Hall, academic and state ceremonies are held, as well as chamber music concerts. Unlike the historical interiors of the Senate Hall and the Rectorate, it is open to visitors.

The **University Church of the Blessed Name of Jesus** (formerly St Maciej's), of the type of the Jesuit Il Gesú churches and presumably designed by T. Moretti, was erected in 1689–98 by M. Biener. The Baroque interior is kept in the warm colours of bronze and gold, which nicely contrasts with the whiteness of the plasterwork. The architecturally magnificent high altar is a creation of the outstanding architect, sculptor and painter Christopher Tausch. The illusionistic vault fresco expressing Jesus' Glory is also an apotheosis of the Jesuits and of the Hapsburg court. It was created by J. M. Rottmayr (1722–27) who also created the superb frescoes in Melk Monastery and in the Churches of St Charles Bormeus and St Peter in Vienna. The sculptures, paintings (including »The Cir-

Ossolineum. View from the Odra river side.

cumcision of Jesus« in the high altar) and the stuccos are of a very high artistic level. Worthy of attention is the marble copy of Michelangelo's Pieta, placed by the altar.

On the square in front of the University there stands a fountain with a bronze statue of a fencer (1904, H. Lederer) displaying excellently balanced proportions.

The corner of the Szewska and Grodzka streets is occupied by the building of the **Library of the Ossolińskich National Establishment/Zakład Narodowy im Ossolińskich**, moved here from Lvov in 1946. Earlier, up till 1811, St Maciej's Secondary School stood here, and earlier still the Red Cross Knights's monastery, the only Czech knights' order in Wrocław, brought there by Princess

St Vincent's Church and the former monastery.

Anne in the mid-13th century. The present building (1675–1715) was designed by a Burgundian architect, Jean Baptiste Matthey, who also designed the similar St Francis' monastery and church, and the Tuscan palace in Prague. Its northern façade, which looks onto the Odra river, is the most interesting, with two projections and a terrace with a domed summer pavillion. The interior, formerly decorated with frescoes by J. Eybelvieser, has lost its historical look after a number of remodellings. An old well has survived in the inner gallery-type yard.

The corner of Plac Nankera square is occupied by the little St Maciej's Church (known as the school church), which was built in the mid-13th c., reconstructed in the early 14th c. (its tower is from 1487), destroyed in 1945, and finally rebuilt in 1961–66. The Romanesque portal, some Gothic stone elements and a fragment of the Renaissance pulpit have survived. The cellar vault houses the tomb of J. Scheffler (d. 1677), a famous Silesian philosopher and doctor, better known under the Latin name of Angelus Silesius, whose mystic poems have been translated by Adam Mickiewicz. In the east the church adjoins the Renaissance parish house (Maciejówka), and the Ursuline Sisters' convent. Earlier it housed the St Clare Sisters' convent, established in 1256 by Princess Anne, widow of Henry II the Pious. The present Baroque building was erected by J. J. Knoll in 1696–1701. The adjacent St Clare's Church with the St Jadwiga's Chapel (1693–99, J. J. Knoll) served

Market Hall (1908), interior.

as the mausoleum for the Wrocław Piasts. Wrocław and Opole princes are buried here, including Princess Anna, Henry VI (the last Wrocław prince) and, placed in an urn, the heart of Caroline (d. 1701), the last princess of the Silesian Piasts.

St Vincent's Church (formerly St Jacob's) is one of Wrocław's oldest churches, and in its present, Gothic form one of the biggest in the town. Founded in 1226 by Prince Henry II the Pious for the

The building of the National Museum.

Franciscans who had been brought from Prague, and built in the form of Romanesque triple-naved church, it was where its founder was buried after he was killed in the Battle of Legnica against the Mongols (1241). His sarcophagus – first located in the crypt and from 1380 on in the presbytery – was hidden in Wierzbno near Świdnica during WW II, and later moved to the National Museum. By then the sarcophagus was empty, and the fate of the remains of the Prince is not known. In 1261 this church was the place of location of the New Town, carried out by Henry III and his brother Ladislaus (later Bishop of Wrocław and Archbishop of Salzburg), in the presence of Princess Anne, their mother, and Bishop Thomas I. In the mid-14th c. the church was fundamentally reconstructed to form a triple-naved basilica with an elongated presbytery and a tower added to its southern side. In 1529 the church was taken over by Premonstrants (Norbertans) who changed its name to St Vincent's. Repairing of the dilapideted building was begun around 1620, its interior was newly furnished in uniformly Baroque style (1662–74): altar, stalls, a prospect for the organ and

The Racławicka Panorama, detail.

carvings, mainly the work of the excellent wood-carver Franz Zeller. Several large paintings by Michel Willmann (Assumption of the Virgin Mary, The Crucifixion, and others) were placed in the nave. The Chapel of Our Lady of Sorrows, founded in 1723–27 by Abbot Ferdinand Hochberg and completed by city architect Christoph Hackner, was adorned with sculptures by J. J. Urbański and ceiling frescoes with scenes from the life of the Virgin Mary. In 1746, fifteen large paintings, the work of Philipp Bentum, were placed in the church. At the end of the 17th c., Claude Callot (1619–87), court painter to the kings Jan Kazimierz and Jan Sobieski and creator of the famous plafond in the Wilanów Palace, was buried in the church vaults. The reconstruction of the church, which was destroyed in 1945 and burnt out together with the majority of its furnishings, was completed in the year 1991.

The history of the monastery is similar to that of the church. Rebuilt many times and abandoned by the Franciscans during the Reformation, it was given to the Norbertans by the city administration in 1529 to recompense them for losing their (fortified) St Vincent monastery on the Ołbin, demolished in fear of a Turkish invasion. In 1678–99 the monastery was rebuilt in Baroque style by H. Frölich from Opawa; after its secularization in 1810, the Higher National Court was placed there. After being destroyed in 1945, the building was adapted in 1960–70 to the needs of the Department of Philology at Wrocław University. Benedictus (named Polak), a member of the Pope's legation to the Mongolian Khan in Karakorum and famous as Poland's first voyager and orientalist, was linked with this Franciscan monastery, in fact the first on Polish land. It was also here, in the monastery, that Bishop Nanker, who was involved in a conflict with King John the Luxembourger, anathematized him, which later weighed heavily on Polish-German relationships within the town.

At the point where Plac Biskupa Nankera square and Piaskowa and Św. Ducha streets converge, on the site once occupied by Wrocław's oldest hospital and, later, by the residence of the Abbots from Lubiąż and, from 1519, by the Arsenał Piaskowy/Sand Arsenal, there now stands the **Market Hall/Hala Targowa** (1908). Its pioneering reinforced-concrete structure and its architecture in German historicism style (R. Plüdemann, E. Küster) make it one of the more interesting old buildings in town. Situated just behind it are the partly reconstructed fragments of the brick city walls with a guard tower from the 14th c.

The Odra river boulevard which we are now walking along is named after Xawery Dunikowski, a sculptor whose famous »Bust of a Worker« stands in front of the State Academy of Fine Arts. From the boulevard and the nearby Wzgórze Polskie/Holteia Hill with remnants of the 18th c. Ceglarski Bastion fortifications, the pleasant panoramic view includes the St Mary's Church in Piasek, and the Ostrów Tumski island with the characteristic spires of the cathedral.

From Kard. S. Wyszyńskiego Street near the Most Pokoju bridge you have an extensive view towards the east: on the left, behind a row of poplars, the premises of the Mathematical, Physical and Chemical Departments of Wrocław University; behind them – on Plac Grunwaldzki square – the architecturally interesting tall buildings of a housing settlement; in the background the premises of the Wrocław Technical University, and to the right, the Most Grunwaldzki bridge (formerly called Imperial Bridge), which is suspended from steel ropes passed through granite pylons. Further back you can see the old brick building of the water-pumping station (1866–71, architect C. J. Zimmermann). Next to the bridge lies the classicistic three-storey building of the Voivodship Offices (1937); its wide, arched façade with a pillared portico forms the northern boundary of the Plac Powstańców Warszawy square. On the western side the view is restricted by the Poczta Główna (Central Post Office) building (1926–29, M. Neumann); its sturdy tower bears numerous radio, TV and satellite antennae.

The corner building at the end of J. E. Purkyniego Street, in Dutch Neo-Renaissance style, was once the seat of the Board of the Silesian Administrative Region (1883–86, K. F. Endell) and

The Most Grundwaldzki Bridge.

presently houses the **National Museum** with the collections of the Museum of Applied Arts and the Antiquity saved from war destruction, the collections of the former Museum of Fine Arts, collections brought from other regions of the country and art bought after 1949. The collection of Silesian art includes valuable pieces of sculpture, painting and applied art from the Middle Ages to the 19th c. In the gallery of Polish paintings one can see works by the most outstanding Polish artists of the 19th c. with Matejko, Chełmoński, Rodakowski, Wyspiański and Brandt in the fore, as well as ample collections of contemporary works of art including graphics, ceramics and artistic glass.

On the edge of the Juliusza Słowackiego Park we see the imposing **Racławicka Panorama rotunda,** overgrown with Virginia creeper. It houses one of the most unique works of art – a gigantic painting (120x15 m) which depicts a painter's vision of the Racławice Battle fought between Polish and Russian troops on April 7, 1794 in the period of the Kościuszko Uprising. The painting, produced in nine months by Jan Styka and Wojciech Kossak with the help of a few other well-known painters, shows the victory of the insurgents. It was shown to the public for the first time on the 100th anniversary of the battle, in 1894, during the National Exhibition (Powszechna Wystawa Krajowa) in Lwów, then the capital of the Austrian part of Galicia. Being of great, universal artistic value, the painting was (and still is) of special importance to the Poles because of its historical and patriotic contents and the emotions it calls forth in the viewers. The Panorama, brought to Wrocław in 1946, and kept hidden for a long time for political reasons, was placed in a specially constructed rotunda (designers: Ewa and Marek Diekońsci; constructor: J. Weryński, 1967). It was opened to the public in 1985, after the necessary, time-consuming conservation of the painting had been carried out. Today it is one of greatest attractions in Wrocław.

Walking along Bernardyńska Street through the park, past Juliusz Słowacki's statue (1983, A. Łętowski to W. Szymanowski's design), we come to the complex of the former Bernardine church and monastery, which now houses the Museum of Architecture. The exhibition showing Wrocław's architectural development from oldest times until today is particularly worth seeing. The church and the adjacent monastery of the Franciscans (known in Poland as Bernardines) situated behind the city walls, belong to the last grand Gothic buildings in Wrocław. The wooden church, erected in 1453 due to the missionary activities and the initiative of John Kapistran, was in 1463–66 transformed into a triple-naved brick basilica patterned after St Jacob's Church. After the collapse of its vault in 1491, the church was rebuilt until 1502. In 1702 a new, Baroque gable was added on the western side and a Gothic portal taken from the already non-existent St Spirit's Church was embedded into its western façade. During the Reformation the monks were expelled from the monastery, and in 1544 the church was taken over by Protestants to be used as their New Town parish church. After being destroyed in 1945, the buildings were reconstructed in 1967 to serve as a museum and to provide housing and the offices of the district conservator of historical monuments.

The **Św. Wojciecha/St Adalbert's Church** in Plac Dominikański square, at the junction of Św. Katarzyny and Wita Stwosza streets, was founded in 1112 by Bolesław Włostowic for the Augustinians and is the oldest church on the left bank of the Odra. The Dominicans, brought from Cracow in 1224, erected a new church here, but it was destroyed during the Mongol invasion in 1241. The church was later reconstructed and extended to its final form (13th and 14th c.). In 1250–70 the single-nave structure with a transept was erected, and in 1300–30 the presbytery was elongated and side chapels were added. The tower, erected in 1359, received a spire in 1488, which was later replaced by a Renaissance dome. The present one dates from 1982. In 1488–1500 the western aisle was added as well as a richly segmented gable. After being destroyed in 1945, the church was rebuilt in 1946–49 (in-

St Adalbert's Church.

terior by 1969). The Loretto chapel, designed and constructed in 1679–81 by C. Rossi, is of interest, as is the Baroque chapel devoted to the Blessed Czesław Odrowąż, the first abbot and legendary defender of the town in 1241. The rich, symbolic decorations of the interior of the chapel (sculptures by L. Weber and F. J. Mangoldt, frescoes by J. J. Eybeviser and paintings by J. F. de Backer) refer to Czesław's beatification. The central place in the chapel is occupied by the altar with Czesław's alabaster sarcophagus, adorned with reliefs.

The Dominican monastery was subjected to substantial remodelling. The refectory from 1724, which has survived till today, is not open to the public. Another Dominican monastery, in Św. Katarzyny Street, which was founded at the end of the 13th c., underwent basic changes, especially in the 18th c. Destroyed in 1945, it was partly restored to its Gothic appearance like St Catherine's

Church. Today both of them house workshops dealing with the conservation of historical relics.

Wita Stwosza Street, one of the streets leading to the Market, suffered heavy war destruction. The classicistic pillared portico and a fragment of its vestibule, to which a pavilion housing a modern art gallery has been added, is all that is left of the once magnificent Hatzfeld Palace (1765–75, K. G. Langhans), later the seat of the General President's Headquarters. The Central Post Office building, which was constructed in 1888 on the site of the old Schreyvogel Palace at the corner of Krawiecka Street, has disappeared completely. Only the classicistic house No. 16 (1804, K. G. Geissler) survived, together with the premises of the bank (No. 33/36) constructed in the late 19th c. on the site of the Pod Złotą Muszlą/The Golden Shell House where Adolf Menzel, a famous painter born in Wrocław, lived and worked.

At the corner of Łaciarska Street (No. 11) lies the former palace of Prince Hohenlohe. Reconstructed in 1924 but then partly destroyed in 1945, with only some fragments of the Empire decorations saved, it has unfortunately lost its historical character.

According to the information available, **St Mary Magdalene's Church** is the second church of Romanesque origin on the left-bank part of the town after St Adalbert's and, certainly, the second already mentioned in 1226 as a parish church. The parish school opened nearby in 1227 soon became one of the most respected in Silesia, after the Cathedral and St Elizabeth's Church schools, particularly during the time of the Reformation. Unfortunately the church burned down almost completely during a town fire in 1342. In the 14th c. a new massive, triple-naved brick basilica nearly 63 m long, 32 m wide and 23 m high was erected on its site. The nave was given a cross-and-ribbed vault, the side aisles tree-pillar vaults; and a star vault was constructed by mason Pieszko over the vast, rectangular double aisled presbytery. In the 15th and 16th c. side chapels were added, and in the 17th c. galleries were built over them. Initially both massive towers were crowned by slender spires with lead-sheet roofs; but in the mid-16th c., for fear that they might be blown down in a strong wind like the tower on St Elizabeth's Church, the spires were dismantled and replaced by Renaissance domes which survived until 1945. Reformation left its mark on the church, in which Jan Hess held his sermons until 1521. After the church had been taken over by the Protestants, the numerous sculptures, paintings and even the old stained-glass windows were removed from its interior. Following the Baroque fashion, a new high altar and a new organ were installed. In 1887 a

Interior of St Mary Magdalene's Church.

dangerous fire caused by fireworks destroyed the northern tower, but it was rebuilt in the year 1892. In 1945 the southern tower and part of the choir gallery fell down as a result of an explosion. After being rebuilt the church was handed over to the Polish Catholic Church. One can still see a Gothic stone sacramentarium, the Late-Gothic statue of the Virgin Mary, a Renaissance pulpit, constructed 1579–81 by F. Gross, and a set of Renaissance, manneristic and Baroque epitaphs embedded in the internal and external walls of the church.

Fortunately, Wrocław's most valuable piece of Romanesque architecture – a superb 12th-c. portal from the Benedictine abbey on the Ołbin, which was demolished in 1529 – survived and can now be seen in the southern wall of the church.

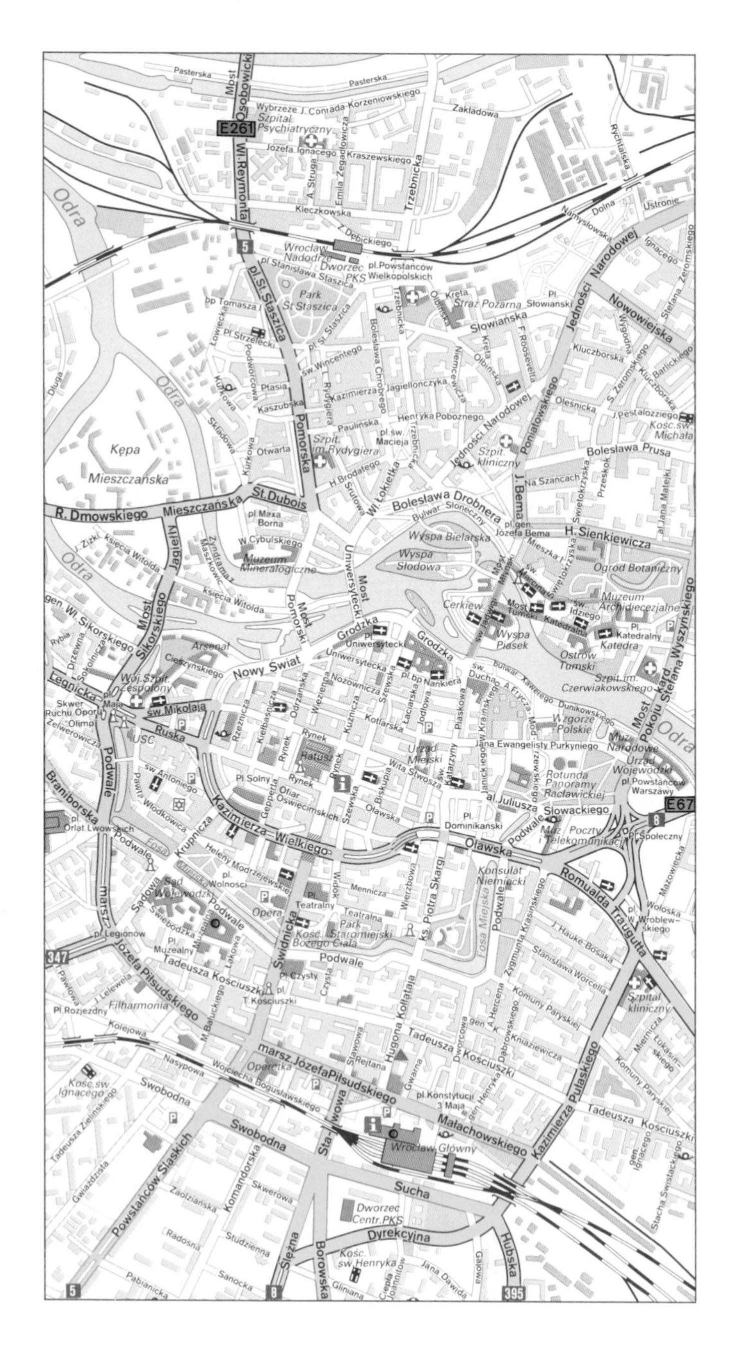

Walk
Wyspa Piaskowa and Ostrów Tumski islands

Most Piaskowy Bridge • St Jadwigi Street • Church of the Blessed Virgin on the Sand • Most Tumski Bridge Ostrów Tumski • St Cross Church • St John the Baptist's Cathedral • Botanical Gardens • Kanonia Street Św. Marcina Street

These two islands, which are the cradle of Wrocław and the site of the oldest settlements, form one of the most valuable complexes of medieval sacral architecture in the Europe of today. The alluring spell of this place, its specific atmosphere and historical past make it a great tourist attraction.

The **Most Piaskowy/Sand Bridge**, which connects the left-bank part of the town with Wyspa Piaskowa/Sand Island on the centuries-old Szlak Bursztynowy/Amber Route, is mentioned as early as 1154. The present bridge, constructed in 1861 with the use of iron, is the oldest in Wrocław. Next to it, on the right-hand side, the University Library (**Św. Jadwigi Street**) occupies the site of the former Abbey of the Augustinians, who were brought here by Piotr Włast in the mid-12th c.

The present, Baroque building was constructed in 1709–15 to a design by J. Kalckbrunner. The eastern wing, invisible from the street, was erected in 1789–1802. After the secularization of the monastery in 1811 the building was turned into the seat of the University Library. In spite of great losses suffered in the final period of WW II, when the headquarters of *Festung Breslau* were accommodated in its basement, the Library can boast an extensive and very valuable collection of books and old prints.

Next to the library stands the **Church of the Blessed Virgin on the Sand**, one of Wrocław's biggest Gothic buildings. The original Romanesque monasterial church of the same name was erected here in the 13th c. as a foundation by Piotr Włast's wife Maria and her son Świętosław. The present, Late-Gothic triple-naved church, 78 m long, 25 m wide and 41 m high, built on this site in 1334–1425, is the third church erected on this spot.

The route of the walk is marked grey in the map opposite.

Interior of the Church of the Blessed Virgin on the Sand.

In the 17th and 18th cs the two Baroque chapels of the Holy Family and St Sebastian were added and the interior was substantially remodelled in Baroque fashion. In 1945 the church was bombed and completely burned out together with its richly furnished interior, including altars, sculptures, paintings and liturgical accessories dating from 1731–32. In the course of the reconstruction work in 1947–49 and 1960–65, the church was restored to its previous Gothic appearance, with a superb star vault over the nave and original tripartite vaults (so-called Piast vaults) over the side aisles. Genuine are the foundation tympanum (1175), fragments of Gothic frescoes, remnents of the lectern, the Late-

The University Library.

Gothic baptismal font of 1450, and some details of Gothic stonework. The Gothic main and side altars in the present church come from various partly destroyed Silesian churches. The altar in the northern aisle contains the famous miraculous painting of the Triumphant Virgin Mary (17th c., Byzantine school), brought from Mariampol (Ukraine). The superb modern stained-glass windows were made by T. Reklewska.

The Baroque church on the other side of the street, formerly the monasterial church of St Anne's and St Jacob's, was taken over by the Orthodox Church and given the name of St Cyril, St Methody and St Anne. It has survived in the shape it had in 1686–96, and is now awaiting complete reconstruction. The reconstructed interior includes a valuable iconostas as well as modern paintings and liturgical accessories. Next to the church stands the old convent of the Augustinian Sisters (1705–15), reconstructed after WW II to accommodate a cartographic publishing house. The ancient St Anne's chapel (14th c.), transformed into a hospital in 1818, is now the seat of the Salesian Sisters' convent. Situated in the neighbourhood are two classicistic houses, Pod Królem Salomonem/King Solomon and Pod Okiem Opatrzności/The Eye of Providence, both constructed about 1795 by K. G. Geissler.

Across the picturesque **Most Tumski** steel **bridge** adorned with the statues of St Jadwiga (patroness of Silesia) and St John the

The Orthodox Church of St Cyril, St Methody and St Anne.

Baptist (patron of Wrocław and its cathedral) we enter **Ostrów Tumski** (also known as St John's Island) the oldest part of town, inhabited from the early 5th c. Here a stronghold was built in the 9th/10th c., with boroughs around it; later, a royal castle was erected and, after the foundation in the year 1000 of the Wrocław bishopric, also the bishop's stronghold with a cathedral in the centre.

After the royal castle was moved to the left bank of the Odra, Ostrów Tumski continued to be the centre of church life – a function which it has maintained until today. When, in 1810, the old bed of the river in the area of the present Św. Józefa and Kardynała A. Hlonda streets was filled in, Ostrów Tumski ceased to be an island. However, it maintained the character of a specific enclave as it was closed off in the south by the Odra Miejska river bed, in the west by its canals and in the north by the grounds of the Botanical Gardens. Although fires, floods and, above all, war destruction in 1633, 1759 and 1945 substantially changed the look of the island, its most valuable buildings survived and are now gradually being restored to their former splendour.

Immediately after the bridge, on the left-hand side, there stands the small Gothic, brick-built Church of St Peter and Paul (15th c.)

St John the Baptist's Cathedral; view from the western side.

and the Baroque building of the former orphanage (1702) with a cartouche bearing the coat-of-arms cartouche of its founder, Archduke Franz Ludwig Neuburg, bishop of Wrocław.

The **Św. Krzyża/St Cross Church** with its strongly outlined main body and slender tower ending in a 70 m spire, really is a pearl of Silesian Gothic architecture. Founded by Prince Henryk IV the Righteous to mark his reconciliation with the Wrocław bishop Thomas II, with whom he had quarrelled, the church was to be a necropolis for the Wrocław Piasts (the prince's sarcophagus was later moved from there to the National Museum). The construction of the church was started in 1288, and in 1295 the presbytery was ready. The building work continued in 1320–50, during the rule of Bishop Nanker, but the basic plan was changed. The body of the nave and the transept were built and one of the two planned towers was erected. The spacious crypt, initially dedicated to St Bartholomew (the patron of the Wrocław Piasts), with a church built over it forms a unique two-storey structure rarely met with in Gothic church construction. Today this crypt, known as the Crypt of the Holy Cross, is used by the Ukrainian-Byzantine (Uniate) Church. In front of it one can see the Baroque statue of St John Nepomucen, a very expressive sculpture by J. J. Urbański and K. Tausch (1732).

The stylish canons' houses (16th–17th c.) in Katedralna Street, which is lined with decorative trees, were later remodelled, including the former suffragen's palace situated to the back (1797), the present Archbishop's Palace and the residence of the Wrocław archbishop, Cardinal Henry Gulbinowicz. Next to it we can see the classicistic building of the Diocesan Curia and the Papal Department of Theology, built in 1795–1802 and later reconstructed by K. G. Geissler (Empire portico in Ionic order) and K. G. Langhans Senior (inner court with pillared portico) amongst others. In the course of post-war reconstruction, fragments of the oldest bishop's residence, from about 1240, were exposed in the vaults, the ground floor and the first floor of the building adjacent to the cathedral.

St John the Baptist's Cathedral is Wrocław's most valuable medieval building. One cannot look at it without emotion – the thousand-year history of the Silesian Church and of Wrocław itself is contained within its walls. This is the fourth church to be built on this site and probably the third after the establishment of the Wrocław Bishopric by virtue of a treaty signed in Gniezno by Bolesław Chrobry (the Brave) and Otto III. Only little is known about the fate of the earlier Romanesque churches. A few remains are left of the cathedral erected by Bishop Walter in the 2nd half of the 12th c. The construction, in its place, of the existing one was started in 1244 during the rule of Bishop Thomas I. By 1272 the presbytery and the two low eastern towers were ready. The cathedral was the first brick building on Polish land. At the beginning of the 14th c. the body of the church and the vestry were erected; the St Mary's Chapel was built later. By about 1416 the construction of the northern tower was completed. The southern tower, begun in 1430, was not finished until 1580, however. The western portico, richly decorated with figural and architectural ornamentation, was added in 1465–68, and the majority of the side

Interior of St Elisabeth's Chapel.

chapels in the 14th–16th cs. The most valuable and best preserved chapels are the Chapel of the Holy Sacrament, the St Elizabeth Chapel, the Corpus Christi Chapel and the Memorial Chapel, which date from the 17th and 18th cs. The spires underwent several changes; the Gothic and, later, the Renaissance towers were destroyed by fires in 1638. The Baroque spires burned down in 1759 and the Neo-Gothic spires from 1913–22 were destroyed in 1945. The present spires with copper-sheet roofs date from

1991. The Cathedral greatly suffered in the various wars, especially in the Thirty Years' War (1633), the Silesian Wars (1759) and in 1945 when, during the siege of Wrocław, artillery fire brought destruction.

The main, western entrance leads through a Gothic portico the gable of which is decorated with stone statues of the Madonna, St Gregory and St Paul. Lower down, on consoles, stand the statues of the patrons of Silesia and Bohemia. The interior, scarcely lit by the light penetrating the stained-glass windows, calls forth a feeling of earnestness which however disappears the moment our attention focuses on the presbytery.

The main altar contains a Late-Gothic triptych (about 1522), transferred here from a church in Lubin which was destroyed in WW II. It depicts a perfectly composed scene of the Virgin Mary Falling Asleep, in which the influence of the school of Wit Stwosz can be traced. The superb Baroque oak pews brought from St Adalbert's Church, the work of carvers F. Motsch and F. Zeller (1662–65), bear reliefs showing scenes from the life of St Norbert, and are decorated with figural carvings. The balustrades separating the nave from the presbytery are decorated with J. J. Urbański's carvings (1727) portraying the gold-plated figures of the Fathers of Church, St Gregory and St Hieronymus. The main, eastern stained-glass window, designed by T. Wojciechowski, presents the two patrons of the Cathedral: St John the Baptist and St Vincent, as well as St Bartholomew, patron of the Wrocław Piasts, and Prince Henry the Pious. Higher up, in the traceries, the coats of arms of the Wrocław diocese and the Wrocław principality can be seen, as well as the insignia of the prince's and the bishop's power.

In the southern arcade of the main nave, immediately before the presbytery, there stands the St Vincent's altar with a bas-relief showing the martyr's death of St Vincent of Saragossa – an outstanding piece of European mannerism created by Adrian de Vries from The Hague, a disciple of Giambologni, in 1614. The altar in the northern arcade, with a painting of the Virgin Mary's Assumption, was Pope Clement XI's gift to Aleksander Sobieski. The marble Baroque pulpit (1723) with reliefs showing the Beheading of St John and St John's Sermon were designed by J. J. Urbański, as were the statues of Bishop Nanker and the legendary Bishop Gottfryd placed on pillars at the entrance. Like numerous Baroque epitaphs, they were made in local stonemasonry workshops. The southern aisle contains a Gothic crucifix (15th c.), the Holy Sacrament Chapel, founded by Jacopo Brunetti (1672) and built by Carlo Rossi, with rich arabesque decoration and a superb wrought-

Presbytery in St John the Baptist's Cathedral.

iron grille, and a Renaissance sandstone portal (1517) with carved tympanum, donated by Jan Turzon. The northern aisle contains the Baroque Resurrection Chapel, a Renaissance tombstone, made of red marble, with a life-size depiction of Bishop Adam Weiskopf (d. 1605), and some relics of 15th-c. polychromy at the entrance to the northeast tower. St John the Baptist's Chapel houses part of Jan Turzon's Renaissance tomb from the year 1537.

Most valuable are the chapels outside the church. The central chapel is the Gothic St Mary's Chapel, built in 1354–61 by the Wrocław mason Pieszke, and has a unique cross vault, supported by three pillars, the Gothic sarcophagus of Bishop Przecław of Pogorzela (d. 1376), and the bronze tomb stone of Bishop Jan Roth (d. 1506), made by P. Vischer from Nuremberg and embedded in the wall. The Corpus Christi Chapel (also known as the Electors' Chapel), built in 1716–24 and donated by the Wrocław Bishop Archduke Franz Ludwig Neuburg to serve as a mausoleum, is a superb example of Baroque art. The chapel was designed by the world-famous court architect from Vienna, J. B. Fischer von Erlach the Elder, in cooperation with Carlo Innocenzo Carlone (creator of the ceiling fresco depicting The Mutiny of the Angels, and of the frescoes on the spandrels), F. M. Brokof from Prague (creator of the altar carvings), Santino Bussi (maker of stucco decorations), J. F. de Backer (painter, creator of the two large paintings Welcome to Abraham and The Last Supper), and with the Wrocław stone cutter A. Karinger, in whose workshop Salzburg marble and local, Lower-Silesian marble was used. The ideological program of the chapel, its interior decoration and symbolism are dedicated to the mission of the Church in the Counter-Reformation. The altar with the Ark of the Covenant is very striking; also of interest are the frescoes in the dome lantern and drum, as well as the frescoes above the door. The crypt under the chapel houses the tomb of Jadwiga née Neuburg, the wife of Jakub Sobieski, and their daughter Maria Kazimiera.

St Elisabeth's Chapel was built in 1680–1700 to a design by G. Scianzi and C. Rossi. The statue of St Elisabeth surrounded by angels (1682, E. Ferrata) in the chancel is made of Carrara marble and faces Cardinal Friedrich's tombstone, which was made by D. Guidi. The paintings on the walls show St Elisabeth's death and funeral; G. Scanzi's frescoes in the dome refer to her life.

On the northern side of the Cathedral lies the little Romanesque-Gothic St Idzi's Church (12th c.), the oldest of the Wrocław churches. A brick arcade over the narrow Kanonia Street connects it with the Late-Gothic Cathedral Chapter (about 1520). Behind it stands the massive Neo-Gothic brick building of the Archdiocesan Higher Theological Seminar. A must is the Archdiocesan Museum hidden away in a corner of Kanonia Street, with superb Silesian sacral art collections, a sizeable Chapter Library and the Archdiocesan Archives. The nearby **Botanical Gardens** of the Wrocław University are a real oasis of greenery and peace. Founded in 1811–16 in the old Odra river bed, in place of the demolished 18th-c. bastion-type fortifications, the Gardens include a valuable arboretum, a palm house, a small Alpine garden, Poland's biggest cactus house and a beautiful flower garden. The

Ostrów Tumski at dusk.

collections of the Natural History Museum situated next to the Gardens rank among the biggest in Poland.

Back along **Kanonia Street** we return to St Cross's Church, passing, on the left-hand side, a building being constructed for the new Archdiocesan Library. As we come to **Św Marcina Street**, we enter the area of the former royal castle. Its relic, the small, brick St Martin's Church built in the 13th c., served as a chapel in the Virgin Mary Cistercian nuns' convent situated within the area of the castle. Rebuilt in the 15th c. and destroyed a second time in 1945, the church was reconstructed in 1958–68, along with other neighbouring buildings. The granite statue of Pope John XXIII has been situated in the square in front of the church.

The Wrocław Opera House.

The Przedmieście Świdnickie Suburb

Central Railway Station • Marszałka Józefa Piłsudskiego Street • Plac Tadeusza Kościuszki Świdnicka Street

The Wrocław **Dworzec Główny/Central Railway Station**, busy and vibrant with life 24 hours a day, is the first place every traveller arriving here by train comes into contact with. One of Poland's biggest railway stations, it is also supposed to be the most attractive one. Its oldest part, known as Dworzec Kolei Górnośląskiej (Upper Silesian Railway Station), founded in 1842 and presently celebrating its 150th anniversary, is now hardly in use anymore. In 1854, in connection with the planned construction of a railway line to Poznań, Wilhelm Grapow designed a new station building, which was erected in 1855–67 in the English Gothic style.

In 1899–1904 the building underwent remodelling work. A glazed hall was added and the rail subgrade was raised to enable the construction of a passage from one side of the station to the other and to provide easier access to the station from the southern part of town, separated from the city centre by a railway embankment three metres high. The two-storey main section of the magnificent, 200 metres long station building is divided by three projections. The central, most protruding one is flanked by two clock towers with an arcaded portico and forms the main entrance. The stylish interior accommodates railway station service rooms and ticket offices as well as cinemas, shops, restaurants, etc.

To walk to the city centre from here we turn left into **Marszałka Józefa Piłsudskiego Street** with 19th and 20th-c. houses on both sides which still bear the traces of war destruction. In this street, which connects the central railway station with the Świebodzki Station, there are hotels, restaurants, travel offices and Wrocław's two biggest cinemas: Śląsk and Warszawa, as well as the Philharmonic. In nearby Zielińskiego Street there is a popular flea market and, at No. 74, the Neo-Baroque former building of the Silesian Parliament (architect Bümler, 1896), today the headquarters of the Polish N.O.T. (Supreme Technical Organization).

At the corner of Piłsudski Street and Świdnicka Street, one of the major traffic junctions in Wrocław on the North-South axis, we turn right into Świdnicka Street, which leads us to Plac Kościuszki

The Central Railway Station by night.

square, the centre of the Przedmieście Świdnickie suburb. Outlined in the second half of the 18th century according to the canons of classicistic architecture, the square served as a place for military drills and parades until the end of the 19th century. Until 1945 the centre of the square was occupied by the tomb of General Friedrich Bogusław von Tauentzien, commander and defender of Wrocław during the Silesian War in 1760. Today, a huge stone placed there commemorates Tadeusz Kościuszko and the heroes of the struggle for the independence of Poland. The KDM Kościuszkowska Dzielnica Mieszkaniowa (Kościuszko Housing District) was the first to be built after WW II (1955–58) in the obligatory style of Socialist Realism. The office building of the Wielkopolski Credit Bank (1910) was constructed in historicist style, whereas the Centrum department store (1929, H. Dernburg) represents an example of modernistic architecture.

The »Monopol« Hotel.

Walking along **Świdnicka Street** we cross the moat and the promenade which was built after 1815 in place of the demolished city fortifications. Immediately after the moat one can see, on the right-hand side, a small 18th-c. guardhouse which now accommodates an art gallery; further on is the Gothic Corpus Christi Church from the 14th c., which was part of the complex of buildings belonging to the Knights of the Order of St John of Jerusalem, demolished in the 18th century. The stylish classicistic Wrocław Opera, on the other side of the street, was erected for the City Theatre in 1837–41 to plans by K. F. Langhans. It was reconstructed after fires in 1866–69 and 1871–72 and again, in 1945, after war destruction. As soon as you pass the Opera, your eye will be caught by the Monopol Hotel (1895) on the corner of Modrzejewskiej Street, once Wrocław's most prestigious hotel, where many famous people visiting the town have stayed. Then we come to the 14th-c. Gothic Franciscan Church of St Stanislaus, St Vacław and St Dorothy with a splendid Baroque interior including Baron Gotfryd von Spaetgen's tomb (1752–53, J. Mangoldt). Further along, in the city trade centre, Świdnicka Street crosses Kazimierza Wielkiego Street, which in the Middle Ages was the central thoroughfare, crossing the Old Town from east to west. From here a few steps take us to the Market.

Japanese pagoda in Park Szczytnicki.

Szczytniki

Agricultural College • Medical Academy • Technical University • Hala Ludowa Hall • Szczytnicki Park • Olympic Stadium

Szczytniki is the part of town situated in the fork of the rivers Odra Miejska and Stara Odra, eastwards of Grunwaldzki Square. Its main axis is formed by M. Skłodowskiej-Curie Street and its extension, Z. Wróblewskiego Street, including substantial parts of the Szczytnicki Park on both sides of Adama Mickiewicza Street. Since four academic schools are located here, Szczytnicki has the character of a university campus.

On the left (northern) side of M. Skłodowskiej-Curie Street and the short Norwida Street we can see the complex of the **Agricultural College,** built in 1915–22 and, in the area of K. Marcinkowskiego and L. Pasteura streets, the complex of clinics of the **Medical Academy** (from the 2nd half of the 19th c.). The large complex of buildings of the **Technical University** on the righthand side of Skłodowskiej-Curie Street, near M. Smoluchowskiego Street and the Wybrzeże S. Wyspiańskiego Street, founded in 1910 and extended after the war, houses Wrocław's second largest academic school (11 departments, about 9,000 students). Immediately after the Zwierzyniecki Bridge (constructed in 1897), on the righthand side, you will find the Przystań Zwierzyniecka pleasure boat harbour; and a bit farther, the Zoological Garden. Founded in 1865 and extended in 1886–89, it had to be closed in the years of economic crisis (1921–27). After being destroyed in 1945 it was reopened in 1948 and, after its extension in 1956, the Wrocław Zoo is now the biggest in Poland. More than 5,300 animals representing over 680 European and exotic species, including many rare or endangered ones, live on the area of 33 hectares.

On the other side of Wróblewskiego Street lie the grounds where the great historical exhibition to commemorate the 100th anniversary of the Battle of Nations near Leipzig and the victory of the Great Coalition over Napoleon was organized in 1913. (Wrocław was thought to be the main centre of anti-Napoleonic opposition in Prussia.) In 1948, an exhibition was organized in the same place to show the post-war economic achievements of the

The Zoological Garden, the Hala Ludowa Hall and Park Szczytnicki.

western and northern territories of Poland after WW II. The spacious **Hala Ludowa**, formerly known as Hala Stulecia (Century Hall), an outstanding example of modernistic architecture, one of the world's first reinforced-concrete buildings, is a dominating feature of the exhibition grounds. Designed by Max

Berg (1870–1947), a Wrocław architect, in cooperation with R. Konwiarz and engineer G. Trauer, the hall was erected in a record time of nine months. With a huge cubic capacity of 295,000 m^3 and occupying a total area of about 13,000 m^2 (usable floor area 11,000 m^2), it has enough room for 18,000 people. The 42 m high dome, supported by 32 arched semi-trusses, has a diameter of 67 m (the diameter of the hall as a whole is 130 m), and a surface of

Central building of the Wrocław Technical University.

6,384 m^2, it weighs 4,200 t (for comparison: the dome of St Peter's Basilica in Rome has a surface of 1,646 m^2 and weighs 10,000 t). Europe's biggest organ (with 222 registers and 16,706 pipes), constructed by Prof. K. Straube and initially installed here, was partly destroyed in 1945.

The original, 96 m high steel spire weighing about 44 t (1948, designed by Heppel), which is located next to the hall, was one of the symbols of the Exhibition of 1948. The neighbouring exhibition hall (1924, M. Berg and M. Mooshammer) and the Pavilion of the Four Domes (1913, H. Poelzig) are now occupied by the Feature Films Studio. Nearby you can see an 800 m long pergola, supported by 140 beams, surrounding a pond, and the park is within easy reach.

The **Szczytnicki Park** (about 116 hectares), the oldest park in Wrocław, was established in 1783–1802 around the residence of Prince Friedrich von Hohenlohe-Ingelfingen, and was initially designed in the style of an Italian-French garden. Purchased by the town in the year 1815 after the Napoleonic Wars, the park was redesigned in the style of an English landscaped park in 1865–67. It contains about 50 species and varieties of native trees and about 320 exotic species, including many varieties of rhododendron. In Dębowa Street we can see the small, wooden 16th-c. St John

The Most Zwierzyniecki Bridge.

Nepomucen's Church, which has been transferred here from Stare Koźle in Opole Silesia.

On the southern outskirts of the park, in the vicinity of the Kopernika, Tramwajowa and Zielonego Dębu streets, there stands an interesting complex of houses designed by well-known German architects from the period of modernism (H. Scharoun, A. Rading, H. Lauterbach and others) and built in 1928–29 for the occasion of the »Wohnung und Werkraum« (House and Workplace) architectural exhibition.

In the north, within the area of the Paderewskiego and Mickiewicza streets, the Szczytnicki Park adjoins vast sports and recreation grounds (about 63 hectares) including the **Olympic Stadium** complex (access by trams Nos. 9, 16 and 17), designed in 1928 by R. Konwiarz, who received a distinction at the 1932 Olympic Games for the designing of the complex and extended in 1937–38 with a view towards the summer Olympic Games planned for 1941 – the year of the 700th anniversary of Wrocław's existence. Today part of the so-called Pole Marsowe (Mars Field) is occupied by a camping site.

The castle of the princes of Oels.

Wrocław's surroundings

Brzeg

Brzeg is one of Silesia's oldest and most beautiful towns. Situated on the Odra, 44 km from Wrocław, on the route to Opole, it was initially a fishers' settlement and a place where fairs were held. Mentioned as early as 1036, it obtained civic rights in 1248. In 1311 it became the capital of the Brzeg Principality. In the 18th c. it was one of the biggest Prussian strongholds in Silesia.

The castle, built around 1296 in place of the royal residence and gradually extended (The Lion's Tower, end of the 15th c.), was transformed in the 16th c. by Jacopo and Francesco Parry and, later, by Bernard Niuron into the magnificent residence of Prince George I of Legnica-Brzeg. After the Piast dynasty had died out, the castle served as the residence of the Austrian princes and the seat of the administrators of their estate from 1682 on. Destroyed in the course of the Silesian Wars and, later, the Napoleonic Wars, it was rebuilt in the 2nd half of the 19th c., but was destroyed again in 1945. Since its reconstruction it has housed the very valuable Museum of the Silesian Piasts. The gate building is richly ornamented and decorated with figural sculptures. You can see the stone statues of George I and his wife Barbara and the busts of the rulers of Poland from the Piast dynasty and of the Brzeg princes – from the Piasts and Ziemowit to the Legnica-Brzeg Prince Friedrich II. St Jadwiga's Chapel, which lies next to the castle, is the mausoleum of the Brzeg Piasts.

In the neighbourhood, on the site of a former Dominican monastery, stands the formerly Jesuit Church of the Holy Cross (1734–39) with a valuable Baroque interior (the high altar, the pulpit, the baptismal font, paintings and liturgical accessories), including frescoes by J. Kubena. The Gothic, basilica-type St Nicholas' Church from the 14th/15th c. is one of the biggest in Silesia. Inside you will find a Gothic altar triptych from about 1500, and a great number of Renaissance and Baroque tombstones and epitaphs. The Renaissance Town Hall from the 2nd half of the 16th c. is one of the most attractive in Silesia. Renaissance, Baroque and classicistic houses are to be found on the market square (partly reconstructed after the war), and in its neighbourhood.

The site of the demolished 19th-c. bastion-type fortifications is now occupied by parks and green spaces with a great variety of trees. Ten km outside Brzeg lies Małujowice village, where the

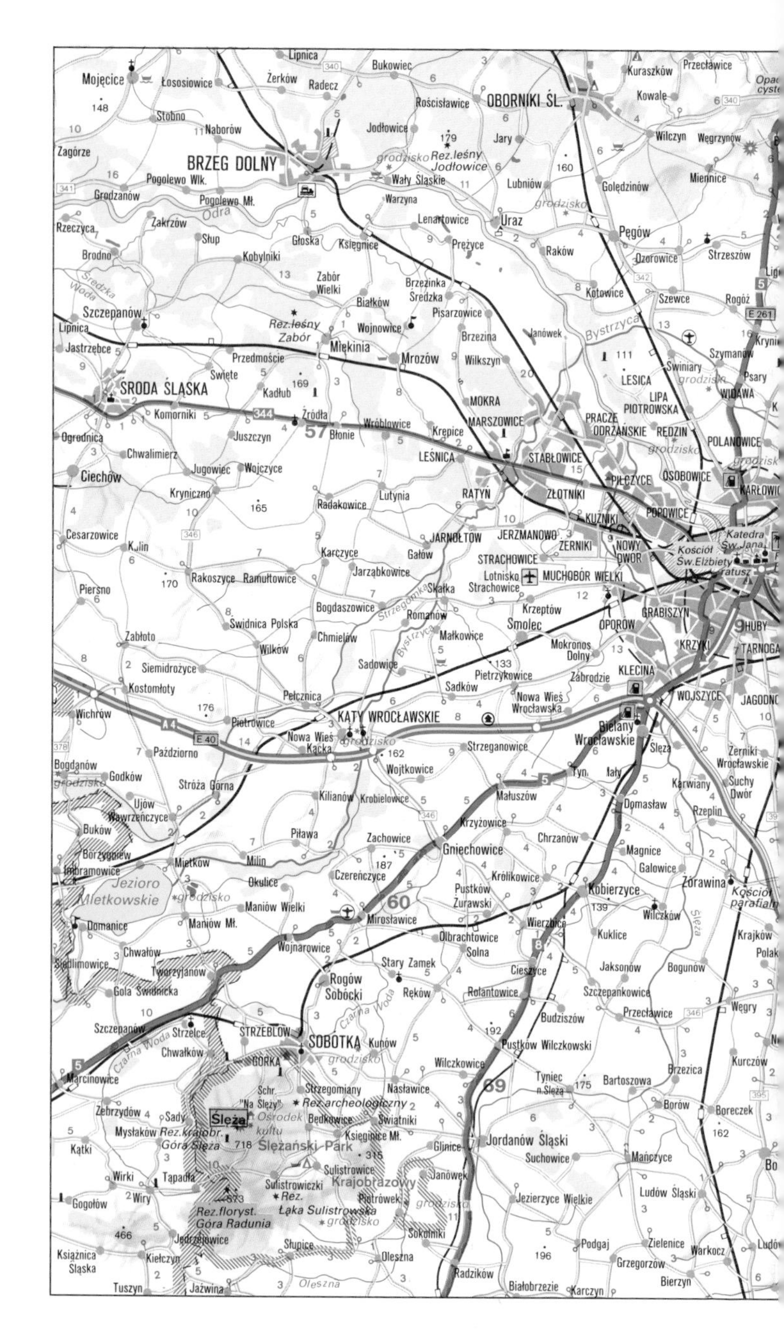

Lipnica
Bukowiec
Mojęcice
Łososiowice
Żerków
Radecz
Kuraszków
Przecławice
OBORNIKI ŚL.
Rościsławice
Kowale
Stobno
Naborów
Jodłowice
Jary
Wilczyn
Węgrzynów
Zagórze
BRZEG DOLNY
Rez.leśny Jodłowice
grodzisko
Pogalewo Wlk.
Wały Śląskie
Lubniów
Golędzinów
Miennice
Grodzanów
Pogalewo Mł.
Warzyna
Odra
Zakrzów
Lenartowice
Uraz
Pęgów
Rzeczyca
Słup
Głoska
Księgnice
Prężyce
Raków
Strzeszów
Brodno
Kobylniki
Ozorowice
Zabór Wielki
Brzezinka Średzka
Kotowice
Szewce
Rogóż
Średzka Woda
Białków
Pisarzowice
Szczepanów
Rez.leśny Zabór
Wojnowice
Janówek
Bystrzyca
Lipnica
Brzezina
Jastrzębce
Miękinia
Mrozów
Szymanów
Przedmoście
Wilkszyn
Swiniary
Psary
Święte
Kadłub
LESICA
ŚRODA ŚLĄSKA
MOKRA
LIPA PIOTROWSKA
WIDAWA
Komorniki
Źródła
MARSZOWICE
PRACZE ODRZAŃSKIE
REDZIN
POLANOWICE
Ogrodnica
Juszczyn
Błonie
Wróblowice
Krępice
Chwalimierz
LEŚNICA
STABŁOWICE
Jugowiec
Wojczyce
PILCZYCE
OSOBOWICE
KARŁOWICE
Ciechów
Kryniczno
Radakowice
Lutynia
RATYŃ
ZŁOTNIKI
POPOWICE
KUŹNIKI
Cesarzowice
JARNOŁTÓW
JERZMANOWO
ŻERNIKI
NOWY DWÓR
Katedra Św.Jana
Kościół Św.Elżbiety
ratusz
Kulin
Karczyce
Gałów
STRACHOWICE
Rakoszyce
Ramułtowice
Jarząbkowice
Lotnisko Strachowice
MUCHOBÓR WIELKI
Piersno
Skałka
Bogdaszowice
Romanów
Krzeptów
Strzegomka
GRABISZYN
Świdnica Polska
Małkowice
Smolec
OPORÓW
HUBY
Zabłoto
Chmielów
Mokronos Dolny
KRZYKI
TARNOGAJ
Wilków
Sadowice
Siemidrożyce
Pietrzykowice
Żabrodzie
KLECINA
Kostomłoty
Sadków
Pełcznica
Nowa Wieś Wrocławska
WOJSZYCE
JAGODNO
Wichrów
Pietrowice
KĄTY WROCŁAWSKIE
A4
E 40
Nowa Wieś Kącka
Bielany Wrocławskie
Paździorno
Strzeganowice
Ślęza
Żerniki Wrocławskie
Bogdanów
Godków
Wojtkowice
Tyń
Iłały
Karwiany
Suchy Dwór
Stróża Górna
Ujów
Kilianów
Krobielowice
Małuszów
Domasław
Wawrzeńczyce
Rzeplin
Buków
Piława
Krzyżowice
Borzygniew
Zachowice
Chrzanów
Magnice
Imbramowice
Mietków
Milin
Gniechowice
Galowice
Czereńczyce
Królikowice
Żórawina
Jezioro Mietkowskie
Okulice
Pustków Żurawski
Kobierzyce
Kościół parafialny
Maniów Wielki
Domanice
Maniów Mł.
Mirosławice
Wilczków
Olbrachtowice
Kuklice
Krajków
Chwałów
Wojnarowice
Solna
Sadlimowice
Stary Zamek
Jaksonów
Bogunów
Tworzyjanów
Cieszyce
Rogów Sobócki
Gola Świdnicka
Szczepankowice
Reków
Rolantowice
Węgry
Czarna Woda
Budziszów
Przecławice
Szczepanów
Strzelce
STRZEBLÓW
SOBÓTKA
Kunów
Chwałków
Pustków Wilczkowski
Kurczów
GÓRKA
Wilczkowice
Marcinowice
Schr. "Na Ślęży"
Strzegomiany
Nasławice
Tyniec n.Ślężą
Bartoszowa
Brzezica
Rez.archeologiczny
Ośrodek kultu
Żebrzydów
Sady
Ślęża
Będkowice
Świątniki
Borów
Boreczek
Mysłaków
Rez.krajobr. Góra Ślęża
Księginice Mł.
Jordanów Śląski
Kątki
Ślężański Park Krajobrazowy
Glinice
Suchowice
Mańczyce
Wirki
Tąpadła
Sulistrowice
Janówek
Sulistrowiczki
Rez. Łąka Sulistrowska
Piotrówek
Jezierzyce Wielkie
Ludów Śląski
Gogołów
Wiry
Rez.floryst. Góra Radunia
Sokolniki
Jędrzejowice
Podgaj
Zielenice
Książnica Śląska
Kiełczyn
Słupice
Oleszna
Grzegorzów
Warkocz
Radzików
Tuszyn
Jaźwina
Białobrzezie
Karczyn
Bierzyn

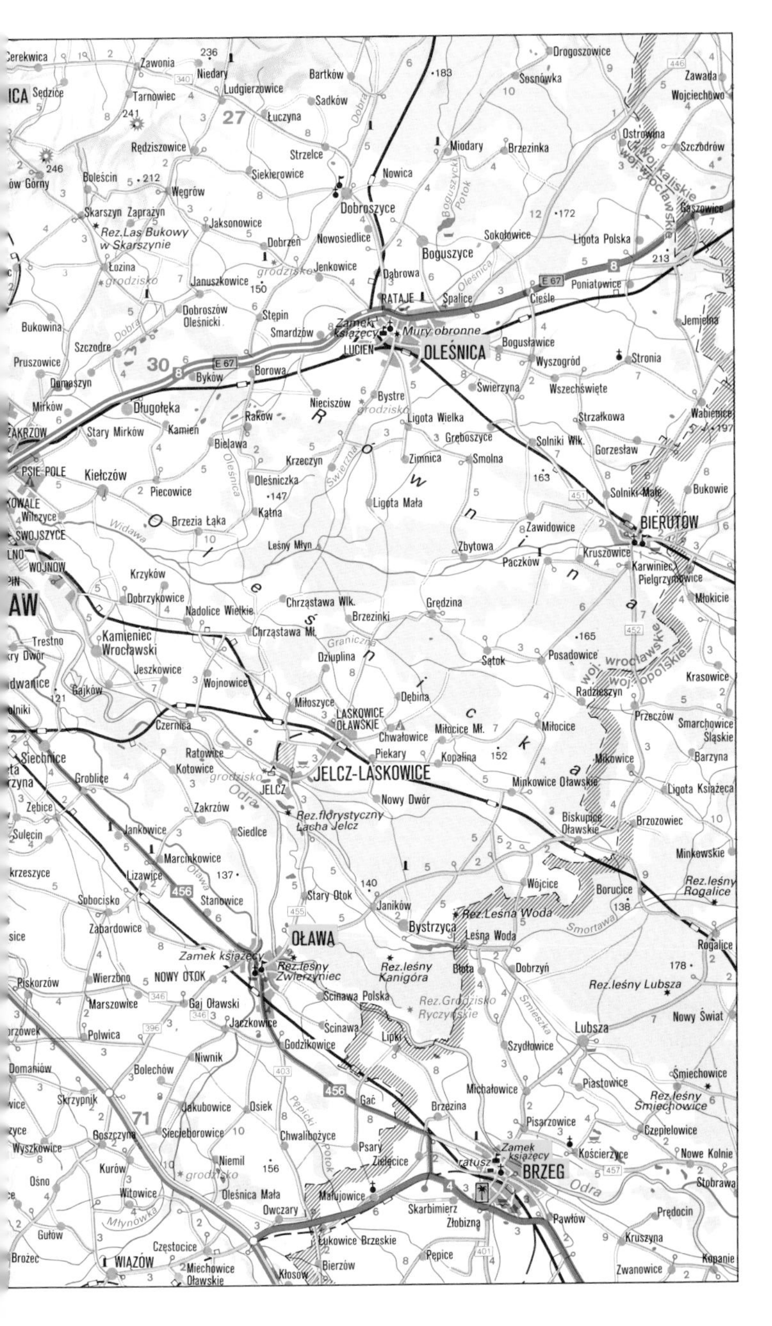
Zawonia
Niedary
Bartków
Drogoszowice
Sosnówka
Zawada
Wojciechowo
Sędzice
Tarnowiec
Ludgierzowice
Sadków
Łuczyna
27
Rędziszowice
Strzelce
Miodary
Brzezinka
Ostrowina
Szczodrów
Boleścin
Siekierowice
Nowica
Węgrów
Dobroszyce
Skarszyn
Zaprażyn
Rez.Las Bukowy w Skarszynie
Jaksonowice
Dobrzeń
Nowosiedlice
Boguszyce
Sokołowice
Ligota Polska
Łozina
grodzisko
Januszkowice
Jenkowice
Dąbrowa
Poniatowice
Cieśle
RATAJE
Spalice
Dobroszów Oleśnicki
Stępin
Smardzów
Zamek książęcy
Mury obronne
Jemielna
Bukowina
Szczodre
LUCIEŃ
OLEŚNICA
Bogusławice
Wyszogród
Stronia
Pruszowice
30
Byków
Borowa
Świerzyna
Wszechświęte
Domaszyn
Bystre
Mirków
Długołęka
Nieciszów
Ligota Wielka
Strzałkowa
Wabienice
ZAKRZÓW
Stary Mirków
Kamień
Raków
Gręboszyce
Solniki Wlk.
Gorzesław
Bielawa
Krzeczyn
Zimnica
Smolna
PSIE POLE
Kiełczów
Oleśniczka
Piecowice
Ligota Mała
Solniki Małe
Bukowie
Wilczyce
Brzezia Łąka
Kątna
Widawa
Zawidowice
BIERUTÓW
SWOJSZYCE
WOJNÓW
Leśny Młyn
Zbytowa
Paczków
Kruszowice
Karwiniec
Pielgrzymowice
Krzyków
Dobrzykowice
Chrząstawa Wlk.
Gręszka
Brzezinki
Nadolice Wielkie
Młokicie
Chrząstawa Mł.
Trestno
Kamieniec Wrocławski
Dziuplina
Sątok
Posadowice
woj. wrocławskie
woj. opolskie
Krasowice
Jeszkowice
Radzieszyn
Gajków
Wojnowice
Miłoszyce
Dębina
Przeczów
Smarchowice Śląskie
Czernica
LASKOWICE OŁAWSKIE
Chwałowice
Miłocice Mł.
Miłocice
Siechnice
Ratowice
Piekary
Kopalina
Barzyna
Kotowice
Mikowice
Groblice
JELCZ-LASKOWICE
JELCZ
Minkowice Oławskie
Ligota Książęca
Nowy Dwór
Żębice
Zakrzów
Rez.florystyczny Łacha Jelcz
Biskupice Oławskie
Brzozowiec
Sulęcin
Jankowice
Siedlce
Minkowskie
Marcinkowice
Krzeszyce
Lizawice
Wójcice
Rez.leśny Rogalice
Stary Otok
Boruchice
Sobocisko
Stanowice
Janików
Rez.Leśna Woda
Smortawa
Żabardowice
OŁAWA
Bystrzyca
Leśna Woda
Rogalice
Zamek książęcy
Rez.leśny Zwierzyniec
Rez.leśny Kanigóra
Błota
Dobrzyń
Piskorzów
Wierzbno
NOWY OTOK
Rez.leśny Lubsza
Marszowice
Gaj Oławski
Ścinawa Polska
Rez.Grodzisko Ryczyńskie
Nowy Świat
Polwica
Jaczkowice
Ścinawa
Lipki
Lubsza
Godzikowice
Szydłowice
Niwnik
Domaniów
Bolechów
Michałowice
Piastowice
Śmiechowice
Skrzypnik
Rez.leśny Śmiechowice
Jakubowice
Osiek
Gać
Brzezina
Pisarzowice
71
Boszczyna
Siecieborowice
Chwalibożyce
Czepielowice
Wyszkowice
Psary
Zamek książęcy
ratusz
Kościerzyce
Nowe Kolnie
Niemil
Zielęcice
BRZEG
Stobrawa
Kurów
Ośno
Witowice
Oleśnica Mała
Małujowice
Odra
Owczary
Skarbimierz
Predocin
Młynówka
Żłobizna
Pawłów
Gułów
Kruszyna
Częstocice
Łukowice Brzeskie
Brożec
WIĄZÓW
Miechowice Oławskie
Bierzów
Pępice
Kłosów
Zwanowice
Kopanie

The castle of the princes of Legnica-Brzeski with St Jadwiga's Chapel.

battle between von Schwerin's Prussian troops and the Austrian army commanded by von Neippberg which decided the future of Silesia was fought in 1741 . In the village you will find a Gothic 14th-c. church with valuable polychromy.

Trzebnica

Trzebnica is a little town with about 12,000 inhabitants, situated in the picturesque moraine hills of Wzgórza Trzebnickie, 24 km north of Wrocław, on the road to Poznań. A centre of vegetable and fruit growing, it is also known as the site of a hospital which specializes in the replantation, surgery and microsurgery of the limbs.

Trzebnica is one of Silesia's oldest settlements – it was mentioned as early as 1138 as a small market village. In 1149 it was owned by Prince Ladislaus II. In 1202 Henry I the Bearded, who was married to Jadwiga (Hedwig) von Andechs, founded Silesia's first convent, for the Cistercian nuns brought from Bamberg. In 1250 civic rights were granted to Trzebnica by Henry III the White. After St Jadwiga was canonized and made the patroness of Si-

St Bartholomew's Basilica in Trzebnica.

lesia (1257), Trzebnica developed into a place of pilgrimage. Destroyed during the Hussite Wars in the 15th c. and the Thirty Years' War in the 17th c., it owes its economic development in the 19th c. to the construction of railway lines (both standard and narrow-gauge) to Wrocław, for which it has become a popular summer holiday resort.

The St Bartholomew's Church (18th c.) contains remnants of two older churches – of a Romanesque church from the 13th c. and of a Gothic one. Its superb interior dates from the 1st half of the 18th c. The high altar, the pulpit and several sculptures in the side altars were made by F. J. Mangoldt (ca. 1745). The paintings, presenting The Virgin Mary's Assumption and The Holy Trinity are the works of F. K. Bentum, who also painted the large canvasses showing The Death of St Jadwiga and St Gertrude. Situated in the presbytery are the marble sarcophagus of Prince Henry I the Bearded (d. 1238) and the tomb of Ludwig von Feuchtwangen, the Grand Master of the Teutonic Knights' Order (ca. 1680). Among the 15 side altars special mention has to be made of St Bernard's altar with the painting entitled St Bernard's Vision, and St Benedict's altar with St Benedict's Death, the work of Silesia's most outstanding painter, Michael Willmann. In St Jadwiga's Chapel you will find a magnificent tomb with marble sarcophagus and a full-scale alabaster statue of St Jadwiga in royal dress. The chapel altar contains a tabernacle with the relics of the saint. The walls of the nave are decorated with 19 paintings of scenes from her life referring to the famous medieval St Jadwiga's Legend. In the neighbourhood lies a monasterial complex, one of the largest in Poland, built on the site of an earlier Gothic church in 1697–1726. At the beginning of the 19th c., after secularization, the monastery was transformed into a spinning mill. In 1870 the church was bought up by the Order of the Knights of Malta and turned into a hospital. Since 1889 the monastery has been in the hands of St Charles Boromeus' Sisters of Charity.

Oleśnica

Situated in the lowlands 30 km north-east of Wrocław, on the road and the railway line to Warsaw, Oleśnica is one of the oldest settlements in Silesia. It is mentioned in a document from 1189 and was granted civic rights in 1245. In 1247 Oleśnica was the seat of the principality administrator. In 1320–1752 it was the capital of the Oleśnica Principality, initially ruled by Piasts, from 1495 by the

The Town Hall of Brzeg on the Market.

Czech princes of Podiebrady and from 1647 on by the Württemberg princes.

The originally Gothic (13th c.) castle was reconstructed in North-Italian Renaissance style in the 16th c. to the designs of Bernard Niuron of Lugano. It survived in a relatively good condition and is now used, among others, by the Archeological Museum. The Renaissance gate is adorned with sculptures and bas-reliefs showing motifs from the owners' coats of arms. The stylish arcaded inner court is worth seeing. A roofed porch connects the castle with St John the Baptist's Church (14th c., tower 16th c.). The valuable interior accessories from various epochs include a masterly carved pulpit in mannerist style (1605), the Renaissance tombs of George of Podiebrady (1554) and Prince Jan Szydłowiecki and his wife Krystyna (1557). On the market square stand the Town Hall (reconstructed in 1964) and a few 18th-c. burgher houses. The Gothic double church (presently Orthodox) was formed in 1505 through the union of two 14th-c. monasterial churches: the Augustinian St George's and the Benedictine Church of the Blessed Virgin.

The Baroque Holy Trinity Church (1738–44) is also of interest. The 15th-c. synagogue was changed into an arsenal at the end of

The Ślęża mountain, seen from the north.

the 16th c. and later, in 1696, into a Protestant church. Large parts of the medieval brick defensive walls and the Brama Wrocławska/Wrocław Gate tower (14th c.) have survived.

Sobótka

This little town 31 km south-west of Wrocław is situated at the foot of the Ślęża mountain (718 m above sea level), which is completely forested, dominating the Silesian Lowland landscape.

Sobótka is the centre of the Ślężański Park Narodowy/Ślęża National Park with good tourist facilities. It is one of the oldest settlements in Silesia, and was connected to the Augustinian monastery in the 12th c. Receiving civic rights in 1221, it was mainly known as a market town. Destroyed several times by wars and natural disasters it lost a majority of its old houses in a fire in 1730, for example. In the 19th c., after the construction of the Wrocław-Świdnica railway line, Sobótka became a favourite summer resort of the Wroclavians.

In its centre, which has maintained the layout of an old market village, stands St Jacob's Church from the 15th c., erected on the

Wayside shrine in the Ślęża region.

site of a Romanesque church from the 12th/13th c. (among the relics, a number of sculptures). The nearby Gothic St Anne's Church from the 14th c. no longer has a tower, but some ancient stone sculptures have survived. The surroundings of Sobótka, with its diversified landscape, are crisscrossed by a network of footpaths which invite the visitor to walks and to longer excursions.

From the summits of Ślęża, Radunia and other hills you have pleasant views of the Silesian Lowland and, to the south, of the foreland of the Przedgórze Sudeckie and Sudety Mountains. Situated in the nearby Będkowice is an archeological reserve; and in Sulistrowiczki you will find camping and swimming facilities. Around Sobótka numerous geological outcrops of granite, serpentine (nephrite), amphibolite and gabbro rocks are to be found, and you can see cult stone rings from pagan times on Ślęża and Radunia.